BEING A GIRL
Who Serves

BEING A GIRL

Who Serves

How to find your life by giving it away

SHANNON KUBIAK
PRIMICERIO

BETHANYHOUSE
MINNEAPOLIS, MINNESOTA

Published by Bethany House Publishers
11400 Hampshire Avenue South
Bloomington, Minnesota 55438

Bethany House Publishers is a division of
Baker Publishing Group, Grand Rapids, Michigan.

Printed in the United States of America

Library of Congress Cataloging-in-Publication Data

Primicerio, Shannon Kubiak.
    Being a girl who serves : how to find your life by giving it away / Shannon Kubiak Primicerio.
        p.   cm. — (Being a girl)
    Summary: "Living in a self-centered world, it's easy for today's teens to get the wrong idea of what life is really about. Being a Girl Who Serves urges girls to think beyond themselves and to focus instead on how they can use their gifts and resources to serve God and others"—Provided by publisher.
    ISBN 0-7642-0090-9 (pbk.)
    1. Teenage girls—Religious life. 2. Christian teenagers—Religious life. I. title II. Series: Primicerio, Shannon Kubiak. Being a girl.

BV4551.3.P76   2006
    248.8'33—dc22   2005032387

About the Author

Twenty-something author Shannon Kubiak Primicerio is a recent bride who resides in Southern California with her husband, Michael. The Primicerios are a fun-loving couple who enjoy watching baseball, playing Bocce Ball, flying kites, and hanging out at the beach.

Shannon and Michael have a heart to see God glorified among youth. Together they seek to offer practical applications to deep spiritual truths through a ministry of writing and speaking.

Shannon has a B.A. in Journalism and a minor in Biblical Studies from Biola University. She was the recipient of the *North County Times* "Excellence in Writing" award in 2000, and the San Diego Christian Writer's Guild "Nancy Bayless Award for Excellence in Writing" in 2003.

She has been interviewed on radio and television programs across the nation and was recently featured in such media outlets as PBS's *Religion and Ethics Newsweekly* and *Time* magazine.

Shannon's ministry spans the nations, as her books are available in several different languages. In addition to the BEING A GIRL ... series, her books include *The Divine Dance* and *God Called a Girl*.

To learn more about Shannon, or to book her for an event, you can either visit her at her Web site—*www.shannonkubiak.com*—or e-mail her at shannon @shannonkubiak.com. She loves hearing from her readers and seeks to answer all of her e-mails personally.

Contents

Signing Up for a Tour of Duty

I can hear the water sloshing around and slapping the sides of the bowl as He moved from one man to the next. On His knees, in a place of humility—or what some may call *humiliation*—Jesus washed the feet of unworthy men. The purest hands of all gently and lovingly wiped the grime from filthy feet and tenderly touched the calluses that had developed from the wear and tear of life.

The amazing part was that He didn't do it because He had to. People who *have* to do things always do their tasks begrudgingly. He did it because He *wanted* to. He did it out of love. And if you ask Him, He would even tell you it was all part of what He came to do. It was as simple as that. Jesus considered servanthood to be His purpose. He found His life by giving it away.

Matthew 20:28 tells us, "The Son of Man did not come to be served, but to serve, and to give His life a ransom for many." If serving others was part of what Jesus was here to do, and we are to be like Jesus, then serving those in our lives must be a big part of what we are here to do as well.

But most of us, if we're honest, would rather go a month without an allowance than wash someone else's dirty feet—especially for free. We are a reward-driven generation. If there is something in it for us, then we'll give it all we've got. But if you want our time and effort, or you want us to share our belongings when there is absolutely nothing in it for us, then you'd better be prepared to hear us give you a good excuse and weasel our way out of it.

We want comfort and cushy bank accounts. We want popularity and status. Sure, we'll serve God. Just give us the up-front place in the spotlight, please. At the core, each and every one of us is like this. Some of us just hide it better than others. But because we are all like this, the Bible speaks directly to this matter. In Mark 9:35 Jesus says, "If anyone wants to be first, he shall be last of all, and servant of all."

A true servant of God has to surrender her rights. She has to surrender her pride. In reality she has to surrender her *all* as she rolls up her sleeves and takes on tasks that might not appeal to her.

One such girl who stands out in my mind is Amy Carmichael. She was one woman who surrendered her life to Christ and exemplified true servanthood. An Irish missionary, Amy served for fifty-three years in South India without taking a furlough. That's over half a century of service without a break!

As beloved Christian author Elisabeth Elliot put it, "The

preoccupations of seventeen-year-old girls—their looks, their clothes, their social life—do not change very much from generation to generation. But in every generation there seem to be a few who make other choices. Amy was one of the few."[1]

Most of us probably do not have the patience or endurance Amy had. We are not all called to serve God on a foreign mission field, or to serve tirelessly with no break. But we should all aspire to be like Amy in the ways in which she was like Jesus. We should not be afraid to roll up our sleeves and get to work. We too should be some of the few who make other choices.

Opportunities to serve God—and other people—come in various forms. For you, serving could mean teaching a Sunday school class, helping out in the nursery at church, or baby-sitting for someone who cannot afford a baby-sitter but desperately needs one. It could mean going on a summer mission trip or giving someone who doesn't have a car a ride to Bible study. It could mean cleaning your church, a classroom, or even someone's home. It could be as simple as offering help to someone who is helpless. Anything that requires you to give of yourself and give to the Lord is a service opportunity.

Most service opportunities require you to stoop just a little—or sometimes a lot. They require you to be flexible, pliable, and willing to be changed in the process. Most of the time servants must take on a task that is "beneath" them. Washing feet was beneath Jesus. He did it to set an example. We need to do it as a means of surrendering our pride.

No servant ever stays the same as she sets out to complete

the task God has given her. Some bring home scars and battle wounds when their journey is complete. Others bring home satchels full of blessings—many times the blessings are a direct result of the battle wounds.

Almost always service means sacrifice. Sometimes servants are called to sacrifice positions, other times they are called to sacrifice their reputation. Sometimes they are even called to sacrifice relationships.

Many times, service requires moving from where you are to where you would never *choose* to be. Other times, it requires you to move from where you are to where you never dreamed you *could* be. The call to service is always an outward call. It calls you out of your box and onto the battlefield. It puts you on the front lines and makes you vulnerable.

Servanthood, though, is not just a call to action. It is not a nine-to-five job, or a position you step in and out of depending on the day of the week. True servanthood is a lifestyle. It begins with a relationship with Christ. You have to know Whom you are serving before you set out to serve, and you have to know Him well. Communication is everything when you are on the front lines.

And so many times before God ever teaches us to *heed* the call, He must teach us to *hear* the call. He must teach us when to stand back and when to step up. Lovingly He teaches us that the results of what He asks us to do are never up to us. He likes to show us how much He can do with the little we are able to give to Him.

God's methods may seem a bit strange at times. He's not a textbook kind of teacher. He teaches us how to serve by actually having us serve. He takes us through training ground after training ground, letting us minister to many different people in many different places before letting us find a place to settle down—if we ever get to settle down at all. Moses' call to service was a call to spend forty years wandering around in the wilderness!

Sometimes God asks us to walk in shoes that don't seem to fit right and go down roads that are dark and dim. He does this to teach us to trust Him, because a servant who trusts her master is always going to be more willing to serve.

When people join the military they sign up for a certain length of service known as a tour of duty. Signing up for service to the Lord is a lifelong commitment. Your "tour of duty" ends only when you cross from this life into the next and you find yourself standing face-to-face with your Master.

And as all servants do, each of us desperately longs to hear the coveted phrase, "Well done, good and faithful servant. Enter into the joy of your Lord" (Matthew 25:21 NKJV). My prayer is that this book becomes a vital tool in helping each of us in our tour of duty so that we may one day join with all of heaven and enter into that very joy.

Notes

1. Elisabeth Elliot, *A Chance to Die* (Grand Rapids, MI: Fleming H. Revell, 1987), 31.

Moving Out

There are many times in our lives when God calls us to go somewhere or do something. He wants us to step out in faith in a situation that seems extremely ridiculous so He can amaze us with what He does. Most of the time we miss out on these exciting opportunities because we are unwilling to move—or let Him move through us. When He asks us to move, He never asks us to go alone. He asks us to move because He wants to go somewhere and He wants us to move with Him!

We think God needs big people to do big things— famous people like Billy Graham and Elisabeth Elliot. After all, why would He use us when He could use them, right? Wrong. God wants to move among the nations and across this country, and He also wants to move among the people in your sphere of influence. But many times we simply do not let Him—not because we are strong enough to stop Him, but because He patiently waits for us to grant Him permission to work through us. A lot of times He works *in* us without our consent, but it is not very often that He uses us to do something incredible until we have agreed to obey, no matter the costs.

When I think about God moving through the life of one individual, a man named Bob comes to mind. He was an insurance salesman, unconnected with government social circles in any way. His friend Doug, though, had a ministry in Washington, D.C. And Doug challenged Bob to pray and ask the Lord to move in one particular place every day for six months. Bob selected Kenya—although he had never been there and didn't know anyone who lived there—and this is what happened:

Bob began to pray, and for a long while nothing happened. Then one night he was at a dinner in Washington. The people around the table explained what they did for a living. One woman said she helped run an orphanage in Kenya—the largest of its kind . . . Bob roared to life. He had not said much up until that point, and now he pounded her relentlessly with question after question.

"You're obviously very interested in my country," the woman said to Bob, overwhelmed by his sudden barrage of questions. "You've been to Kenya before?"

"No."

"You know someone in Kenya?"

"No."

"Then how do you happen to be so curious?"

[Bob explained his deal with Doug to pray for God to move in one place.] She asked Bob if he would like to come visit Kenya and tour the orphanage. Bob was so eager to go he would have left that very night if he could.

When Bob arrived in Kenya, he was appalled by the poverty and the lack of basic health care. Upon returning to Washington, he couldn't get the place out of his mind. He began to write large pharmaceutical companies, describing to them the vast need he had seen. He reminded them that every year they would throw away large amounts of medical supplies that went unsold. "Why not send them to this place in Kenya?" he asked.

And some of them did. The orphanage received more than a million dollars' worth of medical supplies.

The woman called Bob up and said, "Bob, this is amazing! We've had the most phenomenal gifts because of the letters you wrote. We would like to fly you back over and have a big party. Will you come?"

So Bob flew back to Kenya. While he was there, the president of Kenya came to the celebration because it was the largest orphanage in the country, and offered to take Bob on a tour of Nairobi, the capital city. In the course of the tour they saw a prison. Bob asked about a group of prisoners there.

"They're political prisoners," he was told.

"That's a bad idea," Bob said brightly. "You should let them out." Bob finished the tour and flew back home. Sometime later, Bob received a phone call from the State Department of the United States government:

"Is this Bob?"

"Yes."

"Were you just in Kenya?"

"Yes."

"Did you make any statements to the president about any political prisoners?"

"Yes."

"What did you say?"

"I told him he should let them out."

The State Department official explained that the department had been working for years to get the release of these prisoners, to no avail. Normal diplomatic channels and political maneuverings had led to a dead end. But now the prisoners had been released, and the State Department was told it had been largely because of ... Bob. So the government was calling to say thanks.

Several months later, the president of Kenya made a phone call to Bob. He was going to rearrange his government and select a new cabinet. Would Bob be willing to fly over and pray for him for three days while he worked on this very important task?

So Bob—who was not politically connected at all—boarded a plane once more and flew back to Kenya, where he prayed and asked God to give wisdom for the leader of the nation as he selected his government.[1]

All of this happened because one man asked God to move and was willing to move with Him. Sometimes the call to go is preceded by the call to pray. There came a time when Michael (my husband) and I asked the Lord to "give us the nations" and broaden our horizons. And within a few short months we had been invited to speak internationally and two of my books were translated into another language and sold halfway across the world. Our call to go, much like Bob's, began with a call to pray.

Perhaps you have sensed lately that God has been burdening you to pray for some type of movement somewhere. Be ready—He just might ask you to be part of that movement! Take the "Bob challenge" and pray every day for six months that God would move in one particular place—or person—and see what happens.

If you have absolutely no clue about how God might want to use you, then ask Him for direction. After all, He does promise countless times in Scripture to guide us and direct us. Psalm 32:8 says, "I will instruct you and teach you in the way which you should go; I will counsel you with My eye upon you." That means God will not only tell us where He would have us go, but He will also keep His watchful and protective eye on us as we boldly move forward in faith. What a comfort that can be when the places He asks us to venture into seem scary and intimidating!

YOU'VE GOTTA KNOW WHERE TO GO BEFORE YOU CAN GET THERE

We need to learn to faithfully *listen* to God if we want to become faithful servants of Him. In each of our lives there will come a time—and most likely many times—when the Lord will come to us and simply say, "Go." There are specific places God wants us to be at certain times so that

He can use us—and even bless us—in ways that are specific to that particular location.

But that is no reason to freak out over every little detail of life. It is simply a reminder that we need to listen. Before we can ever know *how* we are to serve God, we must first come to learn *where* we are to serve God. Sometimes the answer is not a place, but a process. Like a soldier who attends boot camp in one place, gets stationed in another, and then gets deployed to yet another location, God likes to move His troops around too. Even when we know where we are going, God can change our direction in a split second.

Sure, we can have a general calling—like knowing we are called to work with kids. But we cannot know how that calling is going to be fulfilled until we know where it is we are called to go. And the truth is, fulfilling that calling to its fullest might require that we go and serve God in many different places throughout our lifetime. We gain more experience in every place we go and in every way we serve. Sometimes God calls us to certain places to educate and prepare us for the place He wants us to ultimately end up.

God could tell you to go to one of countless places. Nothing is impossible for Him. It could be as simple as attending a Christian club or going to a school event you weren't planning on attending and meeting someone you wouldn't have otherwise met. It might be sitting in a certain seat on the school bus and getting to know someone who desperately needs Jesus. There are times, though, when the command to *go* is just a little bigger than that.

Sometimes He tells His children to *go* out into the mission field. Perhaps that is a calling you believe God has on your life. Other times, God tells His children to *go* home from the mission field because their time of service there is done. At times God's call to go, or come home, isn't followed by a clear reason for why the call came. But the biblical accounts of God telling His children to go are countless.

In Joshua 1:2 He tells Joshua: "Moses My servant is dead; now therefore arise, cross this Jordan, you and all this people, to the land which I am giving to them, to the sons of Israel."

Where to Go in the Everyday Decisions

Maybe you are currently debating over where to go to college, or you are seeking God's will about where to go on a mission trip. Perhaps your parents are divorced and you are considering moving in with your other parent. I know girls who have recently been in all three of those situations.

When they came to me for advice, I told them to listen for the voice of the Lord. Slowly, one by one, they began to receive their answers—their marching orders—to pack up their bags and go. The practice of listening to the voice of the Lord created an intimacy and trust that made the difficult parts of their moves easier than they would have been had they ventured out *without* hearing God's voice. When we know God is calling us to go somewhere, we never feel like we are going alone.

God's command to *go* does not always involve physically moving. Sometimes it may mean stepping up and *not going* somewhere. It might mean refusing to go to a party where drugs, drinking, and other forms of compromise will be taking place. Maybe it means *not going* on a date with a guy who is unsaved or isn't that strong in his walk with the Lord. It might even mean declining acceptance into a college that would transplant you right into party central itself.

For Esther, God's command to *go* meant risking her life and going before the king so that her people might be saved from death. Her walk of obedience was a short one—down the palace hallways—but it could have been quite costly to her.

For my friend Megan it meant taking a step of faith during her senior year, inviting other Christians she knew on her public high school campus to have worship in the back of her truck in the school parking lot before school started each morning.

Megan brought her guitar, and before she and her friends knew it, there was a group of unsaved kids crowding around Megan's truck "just to listen." What an incredible way to make an impact on those around her. She didn't have to go very far from home to make a difference.

We sell ourselves short when we believe only missionaries can make a huge impact for Christ. My friend "Kaitlyn" (not her real name) has been so focused on becoming a foreign missionary like Amy Carmichael that she has completely missed opportunities in the mission field around her!

So many of us make this costly mistake without even realizing it.

Can I Be Hearing This Right?

Where is God telling you to *go* (or maybe stay) right now? What is He telling you to do? How is He asking you to serve Him with your life at this moment? Sometimes God's calls to us are seemingly simple. *Yes, Lord, I can teach a Sunday school class or go on a summer mission trip with the youth group,* we think. *Those are things I can handle.*

Other times He calls us to do things that sound ridiculous. And more often than not, when He calls us to do something ridiculous, we begin to worry about what people are going to think. Most of the time our fears are justifiable. We don't want to be the girl who stands up and tells some of the popular people at school that their lifestyles of compromise are slowly bringing their souls to ruin.

And we most certainly don't want to be the girl who has to explain why she cannot go out with Mr. Hot-and-Popular just because he isn't a Christian. But secretly, deep down inside, we always admire the other girls who do stand up for what is right, and we desperately wish we had that courage. In this moment, that courage is yours for the taking. God promises to go with you—you just have to be willing to step up and go when He sends you out.

True service to the Lord is a combination of two things: faith and submission. And they work together. If we don't have enough of one, we often don't have enough of the other either. It takes an incredible amount of faith to serve the Lord because most of the time when He says to *go*, we have no idea what will happen along the way.

TAKING RISKS

A few nights ago I was sitting at my desk, working at my computer and sipping apple cider. As I reached for my mug I happened to read what was written on it for the first time in years. It said: *Faith is risking what is for what is yet to be. It's taking small steps, knowing they lead to bigger ones.*

After reading that I couldn't just continue what I had been doing. I sat for a moment and pondered its message. *Faith is risking what is for what is yet to be* ... Hmm ... *What is* could be a lot of things. It could be popularity, security, stability, friendships, or a relationship with a certain guy.

What is God asking you to risk? Even the most adventurous of us don't really like risk. We'd rather be comfortable. We'd rather play it safe. We'd rather be protected. But someone wise recently told me, "God likes risk because risk involves faith, and faith is God's business."

Sometimes it is extremely hard to risk *what is* for *what is yet to be* because we do not know what the *yet to be* is exactly. We like guarantees and bottom lines. We like familiar things, secure things, and definite things. We live in a world that operates on schedules and contracts so we can always be sure about what is going to happen and when.

You go to school and know what classes you need to take in order to graduate. You know what classes will get you into what colleges, and what colleges will best help you to pursue certain sports scholarships or professions. We are people who plan. Even procrastinators are people who plan—they just plan to get it done *eventually*.

But life is like two mountains and a bridge. One mountain is today, and the other is tomorrow. And each day we have to walk across the bridge of risk in order to get to the next day. Waking up and stepping out of bed is a risk. Getting in a car and driving down the road is a risk. Reaching out to people and establishing friendships is a risk.

So the question is not whether or not we take risks in our lives. The question is: What are we risking our lives for? Is your life a series of pointless risks? Do you run across the bridge of risk every day with absolutely nothing of value waiting

> *What are we risking our lives for?*

for you on the mountaintop of tomorrow? Do you ever *live* on that bridge you cross? Do you just simply let life happen to you, or do you listen for the voice that says, "Go"?

Isaiah 30:21 says: "And your ears will hear a voice behind you, 'This is the way, walk in it,' whenever you turn to the right or to the left." When was the last time *you* heard that voice?

When Michael and I were dating, he spent a semester

away at a Bible college in Israel—well, he spent *almost* an entire semester there. God chose to call him back home to the States a little early. Here's what happened.

About a month before Michael was due to come home, he sat in the terminal at Ben Gurion Airport in Tel Aviv getting ready to go on a weekend jaunt to Greece with some classmates, and butterflies began to dance in his stomach. He watched everyone around him laugh and joke with one another as they prepared to board the plane.

He held his cell phone in his hands and ran his thumb over the caller ID screen. *Lord, what do I do?* His prayer was silent, but his soul seemed to be screaming at him. God had shown him clearly in his quiet time that morning that he was to come home and tend to a few things there. But he wanted to take one more trip. Greece was his last foreign adventure, he promised himself and God. After Greece he would go home.

Meanwhile, I was back in the United States talking with our friend Bryan. With danger increasing for Americans in the midst of Yasser Arafat's looming death, we both thought it was time for Michael to come home. Judging by the warnings being issued from the U.S. Embassy, they agreed with us.

So I called Michael and asked him one last time, "Are you sure you are supposed to go to Greece?" He said yes, so I let it go and told him to have fun and said good-bye. When I hung up Bryan looked at his watch and asked, "How much longer until he boards?" When I told him he had about half an hour, he said, "Let's pray that God prevents him from getting on that plane if we are right and he really is supposed to come home." I agreed—although I didn't have much faith that the prayer would be answered. I watched the clock for the next half hour and nothing happened. There was no phone call, so I got ready for bed.

What I didn't know was that, as everyone else got in line to board the plane, Michael told the ticket lady he could not get on the plane and requested that his luggage be removed immediately. He said a quick good-bye to his shocked roommates and stunned professor and told them that his semester had just ended early and he was going home—not back to their apartment in Jerusalem, but back home to the United States. He would make arrangements with the director of the Bible college immediately, he assured them.

It was late at night on a Thursday in the United States and I had just gotten out of the shower when my phone rang. Startled, I answered and heard Michael's broken voice shouting and crying on the other side of the world. Mind you, I thought he was already half way to Greece.

"Love, I'm coming home," he said frantically. "God showed me very clearly to come home. I was reading about when He told Abraham to get out of his country and I knew God was speaking to me and I didn't listen. I have a flight booked for Sunday—it was the quickest one I could get. Can you pick me up?"

Tears streamed down my cheeks as the news that Michael's

semester abroad was almost over finally sunk in. As we spoke on the phone, explosions could be heard in the distance. God had indeed spoken to Michael in his quiet time, and He spoke to Bryan and me, burdening us to pray.

And what happened from the moment he decided not to board the plane to Greece until the moment he got home was proof enough for any skeptic. Not only did the strict Israeli airlines remove his bag from the plane (without suspecting anything suspicious), they rushed him back through customs with no hassle (and he always gets hassled because of his deeply tanned Italian skin and ethnic-looking appearance) and took him right to a ticket counter and applied the amount of his unused ticket (which was paid for by his school with his tuition money) to his ticket home. The total amount he owed was exactly what he had left on his credit card, so he charged it and two days later I was picking him up at the airport.

Shortly after Michael came home some key pieces were put into place that would greatly shape the next several years of our life together. We decided that the assumed plan of his taking a full-time ministry position in our hometown was not God's will for us, and slowly everything was set in motion to move him back into the secular work force where he could be used in a greater way at that time. Within one week of Michael's homecoming we got engaged, and God began to piece together His amazing plan for us. It would not have come together the same way had Michael waited another month to come home.

But Michael did not rush through his decision in the airport. He had been asking God if it was time for him to come home ever since the U.S. Embassy began issuing warnings a few weeks earlier. Safety was not his primary concern, but obedience was. God confirmed His call for Michael to come home early in Scripture and used Bryan and me (and our prayers) to lead Michael into making a decision that was right for him.

Make sure that in all of the risks you feel the Lord asking you to take, you make wise choices and do not do anything rash. Look for Him to confirm things in His Word and through the counsel of other godly people. We'll talk more about this in the next chapter.

Small Steps Lead to Bigger Ones

Faith is about more than taking risks. The other half of the saying that was on my cider mug was: *Faith is taking small steps, knowing they lead to bigger ones.* Maybe today, as a student, you cannot run out and become a full-time missionary or find a cure for cancer. But you can take small steps toward what you know God is calling you to do in the future. You can go on short-term mission trips or do something as simple as taking classes in school that will help prepare you for whatever it is God is calling you to do.

We're not all called to be foreign missionaries. You can be a missionary on your school campus or at your job at the yogurt shop. Someday you can be a missionary in your career. Maybe your *go* is to simply go and talk to one other person about your faith. But in the end it is all of the little steps of obedience that prepare you for the bigger ones. And that's where submission comes into the picture.

My friend Hana really did work at a yogurt shop. She made an incredible impact on the people working at the Subway sandwich shop next door by simply sharing her faith with them and inviting them to church with her when she saw them at work. She took advantage of an incredible opportunity that many of us wouldn't have even noticed. These people saw something in Hana that they wanted. They didn't all take her up on the offer to come to youth group, but they came to Hana with questions and always talked about how pleasant she was to be around. It was a simple thing really—but Hana was able to be an outstanding example to these people. The places God asks us to go and the things He asks us to do are not always earth shattering. But they can still make a huge impact for Him.

Amazing things happen when we attempt things that are impossible, downright weird, or seemingly insignificant because God tells us to do it. Life becomes exciting when we dare to take risks that count for something. Servanthood truly is faith and submission. It's taking God at His Word and setting out when you aren't even sure where you are going.

But the awesome thing about not knowing where you are going is that you cannot be afraid of what's going to happen when you get there if you don't even know where there is! And you need not be afraid—you need not even know where you are going—as long as you know Whom you are following.

WE DON'T ALWAYS GET WHAT WE WANT— SOMETIMES WE GET MORE

If you obey when God says *go*, your life will become more than you could have ever dreamed it would be. Sure, in the end it may not always reflect the life you would have chosen for yourself, but it will be one that counted for more than you ever thought possible. We all want to be significant. We all want to live for more than we are living for right now. And we all desire to be real. We don't want to be fake or to wear a mask.

If we're honest, we'll all admit that we'd like to live lives of epic proportions. If only we weren't so afraid! If only we would go when God said to go.

> *Where could your presence make the most difference?*

C. S. Lewis once said: "I am almost committing an indecency. I am trying to rip open the inconsolable secret in each one of you—the secret which hurts so much that you take revenge on it by calling it names like Nostalgia and Romanticism and Adolescence."[2]

And that's the secret I am trying to rip open in you. What is the one thing you have dreamed of doing for almost as long as you can remember? What is the one thing that you know you absolutely must do before you die? What is the one thing you have to offer the Lord that will greatly impact His kingdom here on earth? Where could your presence make the most difference?

Many times we make the mistake of thinking we have to have it all figured out before we can start serving God. We assume we must graduate from college—or at least high school—before we are in a position to be used.

But that's simply not true. Many times the people that God uses most are not those who are comfortably settled in a stable lifestyle. Often, God uses those who are out there searching—and moving—because they are willing to go wherever He tells them to go; they don't have plans and agendas of their own.

Leo Tolstoy once said, "In order to influence people, the artist must constantly be searching, so that his work is a quest. If he has discovered everything and knows everything and instructs people or deliberately sets out to entertain them, he has no influence on them. Only when he is searching for the way forward, do the spectator and listener become one with him in his quest."[3]

Serve Him on the Way

Serving God does not begin when you get to wherever you want to be (established as a teacher, an engineer, a wife and a mother). It begins when you make the conscious decision to go wherever God tells you to go and to minister to those He shows you in that place.

I was impacting the lives of junior high and high school girls long before I graduated from high school or began writing books. Sure, I knew in the end God wanted me to go and write books. But there were many other *go* commands that came to me prior to that one: *Go and be a camp counselor; go and start a discipleship group; go and teach Sunday school.*

So I set out on those missions, knowing they would eventually lead me to where I desperately wanted God to take me. And by the time I was eighteen I had begun creating a legacy of service—two girls I discipled began to disciple others, and they went on to do so for years. They told me it was due, in part, to the impact I had on them.

Had I waited until I knew all of the details of the journey God was taking me on (which I still don't know, by the way), or for Him to take me straight to where I wanted to go, I cannot even imagine what a loss I would have experienced. I would have definitely missed out.

Find the direction God is calling you to go—and begin to serve Him as you are on your way. Don't wait until you get there. In Genesis 24:27 (NKJV) Abraham's servant says, ". . . being on the way, the LORD led me." If you let Him, He will lead you on your way too.

Servanthood is faith and submission. And if you cannot serve God on the way to where He has called you to go, you will never be able to serve Him when you get there. Jonah said no to God's call, and he found himself floating in a bunch of vomit in the belly of a big fish. God will go to great lengths to get the attention of His children. And sometimes when He says *go* and they refuse, He chases them until they change their minds.

Is God chasing you right now? Where is He telling you to go (or stay)? Where is your place of service? Why aren't you there?

FOR FURTHER THOUGHT:

1. Where is God telling you to *go* right now?

2. How are you responding to Him?

3. Describe a time in your past where God called you to *go* somewhere and you obeyed. What happened as a result?

4. What are some ways you listen for the voice of the Lord in your own life?

5. What is your definition of *obedience*?

TAKING THE CHALLENGE:

Take some extra time this week to get alone with God, your Bible, and a notebook, and simply listen to the voice of the Lord. Ask Him where He'd have you go in your life. Write down what He shows you and date it so you can look back later and remember when He first showed you your calling.

Notes

1. John Ortberg, *If You Want to Walk on Water You've Got to Get Out of the Boat* (Grand Rapids, MI: Zondervan, 2001), 91–93.
2. John Eldredge, *The Journey of Desire* (Nashville, TN: Thomas Nelson Publishers, 2000), 17.
3. As quoted in Craig Dunham and Doug Serven's *TwentySomeone* (Denver, CO: Waterbrook Press, 2003), 67.

2

Serving Only the Still, Small Voice

In college, I used to love when Dr. Shelly Cunningham spoke in chapel. She was always very animated, and she usually brought unique visual aids to demonstrate her points. During one particular chapel she mentioned that her children loved to watch the movie *Shrek*. One scene caught Dr. Cunningham's attention as she was preparing to speak to the student body. Shrek, the infamous big green ogre voiced by Mike Myers, sits down at the dinner table and sticks his finger in his ear. He pulls out a huge ball of earwax and lights it on fire, proceeding to use it as a candle.

A ripple of laughter rolled through the crowd, while a few girls sat with a look of disgust on their faces as Dr. Cunningham told us to imagine someone doing that in our own homes.

"How can someone hear with all that wax?" Her question was rhetorical and there was a hint of humor in her voice. Suddenly, though, her tone became far more serious.

"When was the last time your ears were so clogged that you could not hear a word God was saying to you?" She let the silence linger before moving on toward her point. "So many of us are concerned with our personal hygiene—we bathe and clean ourselves regularly to avoid Shrek-sized balls of wax in our physical ears. Yet we don't tend as carefully to our spiritual hygiene and we let our hearing get clogged," she said.

She made several other points that morning, and on our way out the door each student was handed several colorful Q-tips, to remind us to tend to our spiritual hygiene and make sure our ears were unclogged so that we could hear God's voice. Dr. Cunningham's reminder was a powerful one for me—so much so that I remember it vividly years later.

For me, it had been a busy few months and it had been a while since I had taken time to listen to God. I mean *really* listen to Him. I took my Q-tips back to my dorm room and taped one to my mirror above my dresser. Every time I looked at it I thought of Dr. Cunningham, Shrek, and how long it had been since I had listened to the voice of the Lord. It was also a good conversation piece—people would come over to visit and want to know why on earth I had a Q-tip taped to my mirror!

HOW GOD SPEAKS

When was the last time you listened to God? I mean *really* listened to Him. In the first chapter of this book we talked about the importance of listening when God says "go." In this chapter we are going to talk about the importance of listening when God says anything at all. I cannot communicate this enough: We cannot *serve* God until we know how to *listen* to His voice.

There will be many different voices that speak to us in our lives, so we have to be able to recognize God's voice and discern it from the rest. When I was a kid, I was always amazed when I went to a public place with my mom. There could be twenty or thirty kids all screaming the same name—Mom—but my mom would never turn around to see what they wanted. But if I called out to her from a crowd, she recognized my voice immediately and turned her attention to me. We need to learn how to recognize God's voice like that.

If we surveyed one hundred people and asked them how God spoke to them, we would probably get one hundred different answers. But there are primarily four ways God chooses to speak to us: through a restless spirit, other people, circumstances, and His Word. In each of these four methods the servant of God must learn to discern the still, small voice. If we don't learn this early on we will be led astray many times as we seek to serve the Lord. Let's dissect these methods one by one.

He Whispers in a Restless Spirit

Many of us would probably claim that there have been moments when we just "knew" something was wrong or that something was going to happen. Each of us probably has our own set of experiences where we felt the Lord led us to talk to a certain person or do a particular thing.

Now, we have to be very careful with this method of the Lord speaking to us because—as girls—we have a tendency to let our wacky (and sometimes PMS-driven) emotions get in the way. But when we take the time to rest and make our souls silent before the Lord, He will sometimes softly whisper to our hearts.

In Esther 6:1 we find that the king couldn't sleep one night due to a restless spirit. He was uneasy; he knew something just wasn't quite right. Since he could not sleep, he summoned his servants to bring him the book of records. Maybe he thought he was going to bore himself to sleep, I don't know. But anyway, his servants brought the book to him and began to read it aloud. One section was the account of when Esther's uncle Mordecai—whom Haman, the king's servant, was trying to put to death—saved the king's life.

The king realizes that this good deed has not been rewarded yet, so he arranges for honor to be given to Mordecai by his secret enemy, Haman. This sets into motion the events that lead to the true villain, Haman, being hanged on the scaffold prepared for Mordecai, and the lives of the Jewish people being spared. (That's the short version; you can check out the book of Esther for more details.) All of this happened because the king's spirit was restless and he could not sleep. He had overlooked something God wanted him to notice, so God kept him awake.

Is there something in your life that you have overlooked lately? Has there been restlessness in your life? Perhaps this is God's way of speaking to you. Recently, I had a writing assignment I was a little nervous about. No matter how hard I tried it just wasn't coming, so I began to put it off. The other night I couldn't fall asleep, so I got up and the whole assignment came at once. God woke me up with His message and allowed me to get it on paper in an instant! That's what happens when we let God speak to us through a restless spirit.

Sometimes our restless spirits are God's tools to protect us from danger or a bad decision. Years before she ever met my dad, my mom was engaged to another man. Just a few short weeks before her wedding her spirit grew restless, and she just knew she wasn't supposed to marry that guy. So she called the wedding off—even though the invitations had been sent, the dress had been altered, and they were already receiving wedding gifts.

Later, when she met my dad, she could see why her spirit had grown so restless when she was planning on marrying the other guy. My parents have been married for thirty years, and we all realize I wouldn't even be here had she not listened to her restless spirit. So I, for one, am thankful that God sometimes chooses to speak in this manner.

Using the Mouths of Other People

Another way God chooses to speak to His children is through other people. Sometimes the messages other people bring to us are very specific with regard to where and how we should serve Him. For instance, God sent Samuel to anoint David as the next king of Israel. He sent Gabriel (although he was an angel) to tell Mary she was going to be with child through the work of the Holy Spirit. God sent Abraham's servant out to find Rebekah and tell her she was to come and be Isaac's wife. And God sent countless prophets—Hosea, Jeremiah, Nehemiah, Isaiah, just to name a few—to warn His people to turn from their wicked ways or pay the price.

Like the restless spirit, we need to also be careful about discerning whether God is truly speaking to us through this method. Sometimes other Christians (or even non-Christians) can come to us and tell us that they know God's will for our lives. So it's always important to take what someone else says and measure it up against the Word of God. God is never going to tell us to do something against His Word. We need to learn how to block out all of these loud voices so that we hear only the still, small voice of God.

For instance, I met a girl whose boyfriend told her it would be okay with God if they slept together since they loved each other and were going to get married. No, that is not something God would tell someone. But good, strong biblical counsel from a pastor or youth leader—or another respected Christian—can be just what it takes to help you clear up areas of confusion in your life.

How many times have you been sitting in church or at a Christian camp and heard a sermon that spoke directly into the circumstances in your life? How many times has a letter, phone call, or encouraging word from a friend come along at just the right time and helped you make a decision regarding which way to go? Those are some ways in which God uses other people to speak to you on His behalf.

How many times have you known *you* were supposed to make a phone call, send a letter, or give an encouraging word to someone else? How often did you actually do it?

Sometimes God uses people we don't even know—like authors of books, pastors on the radio, or musicians—to speak truth into our lives. Close to a year before I got married, I told my mom that I felt as if the Lord had shown me (through a restless spirit) that Michael and I were going to move away from our hometown and minister somewhere else. She nodded, listened, and really didn't say too much. The next morning she came into my room amazed.

She reads the devotional *The Daily Bread* each morning, and this particular morning it was on God sending His servants out to new places to start new things. She said God used that devotional to confirm to her that Michael and I were in fact going to move and serve Him in a different place. Shortly after, without really knowing much about any of this, Michael came home from Israel and told me he no longer felt led to stay in full-time ministry at our church. He just felt that wasn't the place for us anymore. So we prayed about it, and God opened the door for him to take a new job about an hour away—a job which would require us to move away from our friends, family, and home church.

Both sets of our parents were supportive from the very beginning. But I could tell my mom was getting a little nervous about the whole thing as the reality of it got closer and closer. During a time when it looked like Michael and I might even be moving out of state, my mom was listening to J. Vernon McGee preach on the radio. (Dr. McGee passed away years ago, but his ministry is still fully alive through books and old sermon recordings.) His topic for the day was Abraham and Sarah, and a majority of his thirty-minute message was on how God sent them out in their early marriage to a new land and a new place, away from family and friends.

Dr. McGee even went off on a tangent about how the best thing young married couples can do is leave their homes, their families and friends, and see what God has for them in their new life together. From that moment on, the plan to move became a reality. My mom knew God was *calling* us to go and that we didn't just *want* to go.

Think about this for a moment. God used someone who has been dead for years to speak to my mom's heart about a situation that was currently going on in my life. That alone speaks volumes about how God can bend situations and manipulate circumstances in order to speak to us and get our attention.

Circumstantial Evidence

Another way God likes to speak to His children is through circumstances. In Romans 1:13 the apostle Paul writes: "And I do not want you to be unaware, brethren, that often I have planned to come to you (and have been prevented thus far) in order that I might obtain some fruit among you."

Paul was *prevented* from going to Rome for a very long time. God used a closed door in Rome to send Paul elsewhere to minister to other people and to ensure that Paul would write the book of Romans, which is so pivotal to Christians today. God speaks—and leads us into ministry—through open and closed doors.

Michael got an excellent new job—that's an open door. My friend Megan just got accepted into the college of her choice—that's an open door. My friend Mical made it onto a highly competitive club volleyball team in a new town, away from her friends and those she has played with for years—that's an open door.

Sometimes though, as with Paul, doors close for us. Some get slammed in our face. But that just means there is somewhere else God wants us to go, somewhere else He wants us to serve, or someone else He wants us to meet. What doors has God been opening and closing in your life lately? What open doors have you been afraid to walk though? What closed doors have you been banging your head on because you don't like God's answer?

We need to understand that discerning God's will can be like putting together a puzzle. It comes together piece by piece, circumstance by circumstance, and not all at one time. In her book *Big Questions, Worthy Dreams*, Sharon Daloz Parks says:

> As human beings we all make meaning. We search for a
> sense of connection, pattern, order and significance. In our

ongoing interaction with all of life, we puzzle about the . . . relationships among things. We search for ways of understanding our experience that makes sense of both the expected and the unexpected in everyday living.[1]

Look for the relationship between your current circumstances and how God wants you to serve Him at this time in your life. Chances are, there's more than you will see at first glance. Remember, you don't have to have life all figured out before you can begin serving God. So start serving Him in the here and now, because He has you right here, right now for a reason and a purpose.

Get in the Word

The best and most common way God speaks to us is through the Bible. It must delight the heart of God when we open His Word and a certain verse jumps off the page and just rocks our world.

I accepted Christ when I was four, but in junior high I definitely thought a lot more about what other people thought of me than about what God thought of me. I wanted to be popular and I wanted to have friends. And as a boy-crazy preteen I even wanted to have a boyfriend—usually a different one each week. And one night, when I was in eighth grade, I remember sitting on my bed and just sobbing. I was worn out from trying to please everyone else.

For the first time in a long time I pulled my Bible off the

shelf on a day other than Sunday. And when I opened it I found myself staring at Psalm 30:5, which says: "His anger is but for a moment, His favor is for a lifetime; weeping may last for the night, but a shout of joy comes in the morning." I was sitting in a puddle of my own tears, at my wit's end, as I read that verse.

Weeping may last for the night but a shout of joy comes in the morning. That was a moment that changed everything for me. After I read that verse I broke, I surrendered. This is the first time I remember God speaking to me directly through His Word. It

> *What I heard changed my life.*

was the first time I ever took time to listen. What I heard changed my life.

When was the last time God spoke to you like that? When was the last time you *listened* to God like that? I cannot reiterate to you enough the importance of learning to hear God's voice before you set out to serve Him. In times when life becomes shaky and unstable, the Word of God is a firm and steady place on which we can rest our feet. Charles Swindoll once said, "God's Word is like a log sitting on top of the ice of a frozen lake. When the ice thaws and melts, the log penetrates into the water and becomes part of the lake. The trials that come along in life are like that thawing process. They melt the heart and allow God's Word to penetrate and become part of us."[2]

THE IMPORTANCE OF HEARING GOD

There will be a million different voices out there that will scream at you, shout at you, and even speak firmly and confidently to you regarding God's will for your life. Not all of those voices will tell you the right thing. There will be people who will tell you that you need to join a certain ministry or fill a certain need, go to a specific college, take a well-paying job, or go on a certain mission trip. There will always be a multitude of people who think they know God's will for your life better than you do.

> *Give God time to confirm His will.*

And that's when you need to know what the voice of the Lord sounds like—so you can sit at His feet and listen to Him before you make your move. Some of the voices that speak into your life will sometimes be right. Other times, they won't be. Again, make sure all counsel you receive matches up with God's Word. Throw out any counsel that doesn't. Don't rush into a decision or an area of service just because a need arises. Don't try to go through a door that isn't yet fully open. Give God time to confirm His will.

Otherwise you will find yourself overcommitted and making a lot of U-turns. I would even venture to say that you should wait until God speaks to you in at least two of the four ways just mentioned before moving forward with major decisions in your life. If it's God's voice you are hearing, He will do it. Look at what He did for my mom with her devotional reading and the sermon on the radio. There is nothing wrong with asking God to confirm His will for us—*especially* if it involves a major decision.

I used to think I had to take every opportunity I could find to serve God. I soon found myself double-booked and completely frazzled. It was then that God showed me it's not about quantity (the number of different times and ways you serve the Lord) but about quality (the effort and focus we put into the tasks we do for the Lord).

We serve a God who speaks. Plainly and clearly, He speaks. He speaks in thunder, He speaks in burning bushes, and He even speaks into the depths of our souls with a mere whisper. But we have to make sure we are listening for the answer.

In his book *A Gentle Thunder*, Max Lucado says, "God will whisper. He will shout. He will touch and tug. He will take away our burdens; He'll even take away our blessings. If there are a thousand steps between us and Him, He will take all but one. But He will leave the final one to us. The choice is ours."[3]

Do not put God in a box. Do not listen for Him to speak to you in only one way because that is what you are most comfortable with. Dare God to speak—not in defiance, but in encouragement. Invite Him to speak into your life and He will. Ask Him where and how you are to serve Him—and He will answer. He always does. Sometimes it might take a little time for Him to speak. Other times it takes us a while before we are ready to sit down and listen.

Right now, take the time to listen. Silence your heart. Be still before Him for a few minutes. Get out your Q-tips and clean out your ears. Learn to serve Him with both ears!

FOR FURTHER THOUGHT:

1. In what ways has God spoken to you in the past?

2. What are some things you wish God would speak to you about right now?

3. What are some ways you can make time to listen to God?

4. What are other biblical examples of how God spoke to His children in the past?

5. How can God use you to speak to other people?

TAKING THE CHALLENGE:

Ask God to show you someone who desperately needs to hear from Him this week. Ask Him to give you a word of encouragement to share with this person—and then go and do just that.

Or

Evaluate the ways in which God has been speaking to you lately. Has He been trying to get your attention in more ways than one? If so, what has He been saying? Get a notebook or a journal so you can write it all down.

Notes

1. Craig Dunham and Doug Serven, *TwentySomeone*, (Denver, CO: Waterbrook Press, 2003), 97.
2. Charles Swindoll, *The Tale of the Tardy Ox Cart* (Nashville, TN: Word Publishing, 1998), 48.
3. Max Lucado, *A Gentle Thunder* (Dallas, TX: Word Publishing Group, 1995).

3

Gifts Not Tied With Bows

She walked into the door near my cubicle at the church where I worked, bumping her guitar against the doorjamb as she tried to pull her backpack behind her without using her already full hands. With a few loud thumps she stumbled and landed—on both feet—right next to me, huffing and puffing.

"I hate playing the guitar, I want to quit," Chelsea, a high school freshman, said in a matter-of-fact tone. Blowing a stray strand of her long blond hair out of her face, she plopped herself in the chair next to mine and began to whine and complain about how she was only going to keep taking lessons because her parents made her pay for half of her guitar herself—precisely for this reason, I am sure.

I simply listened to Chelsea and don't recall saying too much to her on the topic. Later that night I taught on the importance of listening to God when He speaks to us about what He would have us to do with our lives. It was a message very similar to the one in the first chapter. After our girls' Bible study, Chelsea told me God used my message to encourage her to keep playing and not give up.

Week after week I watched her stumble in the door with

her hands full, a look of frustration on her face. After several weeks passed her frustration became determination, and I could hear improvement as she sat and faithfully strummed her chords. One week she busted in the door, hardly able to contain her excitement.

"Do you want to hear a song I wrote?" She pulled her guitar out of its case as she spoke. "I'm still working on it, but I think I know it enough to play it for you." She sat in the same chair she always did as I pulled away from my desk and turned to face her. What came out of her mouth and guitar was so amazing that I closed my eyes and pretended I was in my car listening to the radio. A few other people walked into the room mid-song and stopped to listen. When she finished she had a plethora of requests to play it again. That night I had her play it at Bible study.

A few weeks later she came to show me her new guitar case, and I had her play the song for me yet again. Finally I had to ask the question that had been nagging me for days.

"Chelsea," I started slowly, "do you realize a few weeks ago you were ready to quit guitar altogether and just give up?"

"That was a long time ago," she said, trying to brush me off. "I got my guitar on January first." I looked at my calendar and then back at her.

"Today is only March first," I said. "You couldn't have wanted to quit more than six weeks ago, because that's when I taught the message you said God used to show you to keep going." She pursed her lips and thought about it silently for a moment.

"You're right," she said, leaning back in her chair with her arm resting on her guitar. "Now I really feel God wants to use me through music and let that be my mission field."

I nodded and pointed out all of the various ways He already was: She sang on the youth group worship team and she was cast as the lead in a local musical. Here she was, sitting right in front of me, writing, singing, and playing songs—which is not easy to do. I reminded her that God gifted her for a reason, and I challenged her to record her song.

God has given each of us numerous talents with which we can serve Him. One of Chelsea's gifts is music. My friend Mical is a gifted athlete. In the years I have known her she has been both a skilled gymnast and an incredible volleyball player. In junior high she left gymnastics to focus on volleyball. She is now a senior on the volleyball team at a Christian high school. But she also plays on a club team full of non-Christian girls. She travels with these girls to and from games, and spends more time with them at practice each week than she does with her own friends or family. As a pastor's daughter it can sometimes be rough to miss church on a Sunday for a game, but Mical brings church to her team in the way she lives and plays the game. She is using her gift—a seemingly unspiritual gift—for God's glory. And that has been God's plan all along.

GIFTED FOR A PURPOSE

God has made it clear in His Word that our gifts—and even our interests—were given to us for a purpose. Your artistic ability, athletic endurance, spirit of hospitality, or your super-sharp mind are no accident. God has a plan for you, and your gifts and talents are all part of how He wants you to serve Him. We serve a God who loves us and wants us to experience His joy as we use His gifts to serve others.

Notice the Bible says, "Delight yourself in the LORD; and He will give you the desires of your heart" (Psalm 37:4).

That's a promise ... if we *delight* in Him, our desires will be aligned with His and He will give us those very dreams and desires. Sometimes when we begin to delight ourselves in the Lord, He will change and tweak our desires ever so slightly. My friend Amanda wanted to major in business and eventually work in international business over in Europe. But partway through college God led her to leave school early and head to the mission field in Eastern Europe. He still let her keep her passion—He just altered it a bit for His purposes. And in the end what He gave her was more than she could have ever imagined.

So many times, though, we view God as an inconsiderate taskmaster. *Oh, He will give me anything but the one thing I really want. He'll let me serve Him in any way but the one way I want to serve Him,* we think to ourselves. And because our thinking is off, we miss out on the blessing of serving God with our gifts and talents.

If our parents gave us a new car for Christmas, I am sure we would not leave it sitting in the garage claiming they don't really want us to drive it. So why is it that we can justify letting the gifts God has given us lie dormant, claiming He doesn't really want us to use them? Many times the ways in which God asks us to serve Him are ways that are fun and exciting. Sometimes they are ways that even allow us to showcase (notice I did not say *show off*) our very talents and passions.

Proverbs 18:16 tells us, "A man's gift makes room for him, and brings him before great men." Proverbs 22:29 affirms that verse and restates it in a different way: "Do you see a man skilled in his work? He will stand before kings; He will not stand before obscure men."

Wow! The first time I realized those two verses were in the Bible I was too shocked for words. A million thoughts raced through my mind. *You mean God actually has a purpose for the things He has made me good at? Yes! You mean He can actually use things like the ability to write and tell stories to bring glory to himself? Yes! You mean things that are not necessarily spiritual gifts can still have eternal significance if they are used for God's glory?* Yes! Yes! Yes!

Many times we will meet people who will tell us that only "spiritual" gifts can be used by God. I knew a guy in college who told me God could never be glorified by my writing books. When we believe that God cannot use the very gifts He has given us—no matter how unspiritual they may seem—we limit God's power and we thwart His purpose for our lives. My life would be drastically different, and I would be outside of God's will for me, had I listened to that guy's opinion.

So many times we look at the lives of the people in the Bible and automatically think that everything about their lives was spiritual. We view them as holy and saintly, not as the regular everyday people they actually were. Having this sort of tainted view rips us off from realizing *why* God cared enough to have their stories recorded and preserved for us to read.

God used the fact that Esther was beautiful to make her queen and have her preserve the Jewish race. He used something Peter knew about—catching fish—to teach him about catching men. He used David's ability to shepherd flocks to teach him how to rule a nation.

So many times we miss opportunities for service by thinking that certain things are not important enough or holy enough for God to use for His glory. Honestly, you can be used anywhere doing almost anything. Sure, some people are gifted to be worship leaders and Bible teachers, but they cannot get up there and do what they are called to do if there aren't people running the sound board and PowerPoint presentations.

Think about how different church would be if no one ever greeted you at the door, handed out the church bulletin, set up the communion table, or ran the sound equipment for worship and the morning teaching. Maybe you are a member of a small youth group where many of these things are unnecessary. If so, picture a Billy Graham crusade and imagine what would happen if no one but Billy Graham showed up to facilitate the event. It would be a disaster!

The truth of the matter is that we were designed to be the body of Christ for a reason. It takes more than one of us to do all of the things God wants us to do. So don't look around at what everyone else is doing. Don't compare your gifts to someone else's—we're girls, sometimes it's hard not to do that. I know. But really, it takes a whole team. So look at those placed by God on your team for now, and think about how *you* fit on that team. What is it that you have to offer? What are your gifts and talents?

Also, make it a point not to diminish the gifts of others. If your gifts put you in an upfront place of service, make sure to acknowledge, thank, and appreciate all those who make what you do possible. There is no such thing as a small gift when it comes from God. In the end, nobody's role is more important to Him than anyone else's.

> *Nobody's role is more important to Him than anyone else's.*

MAKING ROOM

If the verses I mentioned in Proverbs earlier are really true (which of course they are), then our gifts are always making room for us somewhere. My friend Heidi is a phenomenal artist. I always pester her, trying to get her to paint me something beautiful to hang in my house. Not too long ago she spent the summer in Israel, helping out in various shelters, refugee camps, and homes in Palestinian-occupied territory. She has wanderlust like few others I have met, and she travels more than anyone else

I know. When I call her I'm usually not sure if she's in the United States at the moment or not.

On this particular trip they needed artists to paint murals in refugee camps so that the people—especially the children—would have something beautiful to look at and distract them from all of the violence going on around them. Her simple gift of art brought beauty to a broken and devastated place.

My friend Sarah, who is also an artist, went on a mission trip to China. Before she left she had lunch with me and she said one of the things God used to confirm that she was to go on the trip was their need for an artist to paint murals in the orphanage. Sarah was the only artist interested in going on the trip.

You may have picked up this book thinking it was going to make you a better Sunday school teacher, a better singer on the youth group worship team, or that it would help prepare you for your upcoming summer mission trip. As much as I hope and pray it does all of those things, I also hope it does something more. My prayer is that this book stirs a passion in you to do the one thing God has truly called you to do: glorify Him with your life.

That means in everything you say and everything you do, you *serve God*. It means you view the simple act of breathing as an act of worship. Something as simple as offering a smile and a kind word to someone who looks a little lost wandering the halls of your school can be viewed as an act of service.

Doing a science project on creationism and not evolution

can become a powerful tool in the hand of God on a public school campus or in the regional or state science fair. Giving a speech on pro-life views in your debate class could do a lot of good as people are forced to sit there and listen to what you have to say.

Did you catch what I just said? Even your *homework* can become an opportunity to serve God. So many times, though, we don't look for those opportunities. We just blow right by them because we are so caught up in serving only in typical ministry outlets.

POP QUIZ

Come on now, what are you good at? What are your gifts and talents? What is the one thing you can do that people always compliment you on? There has to be something.

> Insecurity is a form of pride.

If you can't think of anything at the moment, it is not because you are not gifted and talented but because you are off hiding in the shadows somewhere—too scared to step out. Have you ever realized that insecurity is a form of pride? We are only insecure because we are spending too much time focusing on ourselves and what we can or cannot do—what other people will or will not think of us.

I have a friend who is one of the most gifted musicians I have ever met. Not only can she play the guitar, but she also has a deep, throaty voice that could probably make her famous. Her talent is truly amazing. In conversation one day she told me that she used to be terrified to sing in front of people, especially her parents, because of how badly she wanted approval. For a while this prevented her from doing things like leading worship, but she prayed through it and several people helped draw her gifts out. Now she serves as a youth group worship leader on a regular basis.

If God gifted you, He gifted you for a reason. Our gifts in the body of Christ may be different, but His purpose for all of us is the same: to glorify himself. So come on now, how can *you* glorify God with the gifts He has given you? If you don't use them, you just may lose them. My friend Amanda recently told me that God gave her a certain gift years ago (she didn't say what it was), but she was so intimidated by it that she rarely used it. She said she recently tried to do whatever it was and the ability to do it was gone.

We grow our gifts and talents by practice. The more we use what God has given us, the more glory He gets. Many times we become stuck when it comes to figuring out ways in which we can serve God. *I really, really want to serve God,* we think to ourselves. *But I just don't know how.* Pray about it. Ask God to open your eyes to whatever gifts, talents, and passions He has given you (if He hasn't already). And then begin looking, and prayerfully seeking, ways in which you can get out there and do something related to them.

The best piece of advice any servant of God can receive is to spend the beginning of each day on your knees before the

Lord in prayer. Open His Word before you ever open your door to step outside. And once you have done those two things, grab your paintbrush, your guitar, your volleyball, your pen and paper—or whatever tools you need—and then get out there and use your talents for the glory of God!

FOR FURTHER THOUGHT:

1. What are some of your gifts and interests?

2. How can you use those for God's glory?

3. What is the one thing you dream of doing for God?

4. What can you do right now that would help you grow and cultivate your gifts? (e.g., take an art class or guitar lessons, sign up for a creative writing course, etc.).

5. In your own words, what does Psalm 37:4 mean?

TAKING THE CHALLENGE:

Find one way to use your gifts as a way of serving someone else this week. Write an encouraging note, paint a beautiful picture and give it away, share your voice by singing to someone else, make a batch of your fabulous cookies to share ... Whatever you do best, get out there and do it for the glory of God!

4

Learning to Stoop

I grew up in upper-middle-class white America. Many kids at my high school drove a Mercedes. One girl even had a Jaguar. I drove a Volkswagen Jetta. Growing up, my best friend was Asian and another good friend of mine was Colombian. But for the most part, everyone I knew was white. I wasn't racist by any means. Sheltered would be a better term. I was used to living in a nice house and having nice things that I didn't have to share with any siblings. Being an only child, I never owned a hand-me-down. I grew up in a safe, quaint small town that has since blossomed into full-blown suburbia.

The idea of ministry I had grown accustomed to was serving in youth ministry in my large church right in the middle of your typical neighborhood in Yuppies Ville. It seemed like almost every family had 2.5 kids, an SUV, and a dog. In my neighborhood the American Dream was not just achieved, it was surpassed. Growing up in Southern California, the people around me always had a lot of stuff. To me, this was normal. The glamour of Hollywood had greatly influenced the thinking of those around me, and that is how I thought most people lived—I know, it was very naïve.

When I went to college the endless ministry opportunities that awaited me took me a little by surprise. Yes, I had been on a mission trip to Eastern Europe with my youth group, but the concept of having a mission field—and a foreign one at that—in my own backyard was very new to me. Moving to Los Angeles—which is a melting pot of cultures—was something I wasn't really prepared for.

After sitting through the Student Ministries chapel one morning and listening to all of the ways I could serve God in my first semester of college, the one place I felt called to go was one place I never thought I *would* go. I felt called to the inner city of Los Angeles. Several weeks later I found myself in the heart of skid row with a handful of other Biola students—mostly girls. And for the first time in a long time I had no clue how I had gotten there.

My first few weeks volunteering with the S.A.Y. Yes! after-school program were eye-opening. My blond hair and blue eyes stood out in the sea of chocolate brown faces surrounding me. Many of the children who came to S.A.Y. Yes! had only one parent. Many did not know their fathers, and some had mothers who were involved in prostitution or lifestyles of drug dealing.

Several of the kids shared a room—one tiny room—with their *entire* family in a run-down hotel that had been turned into a shelter. Their only source of heat was a hot plate, and some would accidentally burn themselves in the night by rolling over onto the heated metal. The burns they would come in with on their faces, arms, and legs were sometimes unsightly. I was at a loss as to how to minister to these children. No matter how hard I tried, I could not relate to them.

When I first started going to the inner city, my fear and uncertainty over what I might encounter was obvious. I would not get down on the cockroach-ridden floor and play with the children. When it came time to feed them dinner I would sit among them, but I wouldn't eat. I was even apprehensive about letting these attention-starved children climb all over me and give me hugs and kisses.

In the beginning my fear was immense and my pride was very strong. I was uncomfortable driving in a car filled with four other girls in and out of a rough part of Los Angeles—sometimes as the sun was going down. *Lord, what am I doing here?* I used to pray. *I don't know how to minister to these children. Send me back to a place where I know how to serve!*

But week by week the Lord worked on me. He chiseled away my pride and He carved out my character. Pretty soon I could be found with one child on my lap, another braiding my hair, and a third clinging to my free arm as I read them a story. At dinner I became just like everyone else. I piled up a plate, thanked God for it, and sat down to eat. For me, venturing into inner-city Los Angeles was like taking Servanthood 101. It brought me out of my comfort zone and into a place where I was fully reliant on God. I was like a soldier emerging from boot camp and finding myself right in the heat of the battle. All I had been taught about serving God in the past came into play every time I ventured into the inner city.

Many times, as servants of God, we are called to serve in places that might make us a little uncomfortable. Perhaps you are ready to slam this book shut without reading any further because your own mind is flooded with all of the places you would never want to go. Often our pride keeps us from God's will. God calls, and we don't want to answer. We would rather let the answering machine get it so someone else can get the message.

Often our pride keeps us from God's will.

We, as people, are very prideful by nature. Each of us hungers for status and power. Deep inside we want to be highly esteemed and remembered for our greatness. All of us want to be popular, well liked, even somewhat well known. If given an incredible opportunity or an awesome position by the Lord, we would never dream of surrendering it to do something else. Many people want to "serve" in the church, but no one wants to be the one cleaning the toilets.

THE ART OF STOOPING

Gregory the Great once said, "Be not anxious about what you have, but about what you are."[1] Many of us, though, are anxious about what we have and care very little about what we are inside. And it is when we are in the most selfish places of our lives that God tends to come to us with the command to take a demotion and venture into an uncomfortable place. He asks us to stoop. Very often our pride is pushed down even further by God as He asks us to stoop to a level we think is "beneath" us.

He comes to us with the call to step down from our prideful pedestals, go to a place we would never choose to go, and serve someone we would never desire to serve. He calls us to do something that is both humbling and uncomfortable. Although God deals with each of us differently, beneath whatever our outward circumstances may be, His methods are the same.

Stooping for you may not look like stooping to me. And stooping for me might not look like stooping to you. But God knows us each intimately, and because of that He tends to handpick the situations in which He would have us to stoop to match the needs we have in our lives. He asks us to step into positions that best allow us to learn whatever lesson we *need* (notice I did not say *want*) to learn.

Has God ever asked you to do something ridiculous? Have you ever felt as if God was sending you to the one place you absolutely did not want to go? The Bible is full of stories about God asking His servants to do the very same thing—to go somewhere they did not want to go or do something they did not want to do. Two of God's servants stand out in my mind when I think of stooping. The first is Moses and the second is Jesus. Let's look at Moses first.

Leaving the Throne for the Desert

Exodus 2 tells how all of the male Israelite babies were being killed in the land of Egypt at Pharaoh's command, and in faith Moses' mother placed him in a basket and set him in the Nile River so that his life might be spared. God allows Pharaoh's daughter to find him and adopt him, thus elevating Moses from a slave to a prince literally overnight.

Later on, when Moses is all grown up, we see that his heart is stirred in a way that no prince of Egypt was ever stirred before. Picture the scene described in verses 11–15 with me:

There stands Moses, arrayed in all of his princely garb, looking very much like a young Pharaoh in training should. He looks out on the children of Israel slaving away as they build the grandeur of Egypt, and he sees an Egyptian taskmaster beating an Israelite slave. Moses' heart burns within him and he waits until no one is around. Then he rushes out and kills the Egyptian taskmaster and buries him in the sand. Not the typical behavior of a good Egyptian prince.

Although the way Moses handles the situation is wrong, we see that his heart is stirred with passion for his true people— the children of Israel. At this point in his life Moses was a prince. He had power and authority and the promise of a future that would be bright and financially stable. But he looks out at the children of Israel and has compassion on them. That's a compassion that can only come from God.

If I had been Moses, in all honesty, I would have probably looked out at the children of Israel and thought something like, *Thank you, God, for sparing me from the misery of slaving away like my brethren and for exalting me to a position of royalty. Use me here and definitely not there, Lord!*

Pharaoh hears of Moses' behavior and fears an uprising. He wants Moses dead, so Moses flees for his life. These are the circumstances that began Moses' lessons in stooping. He goes from prince to pauper overnight. Exodus tells us that he spends the next forty years in the desert of Midian, where he takes a wife, becomes a shepherd, and starts a family. Not the type of future this former prince of Egypt once thought he would have, I'm sure.

Perhaps you have found yourself herding sheep when you thought you should be sitting on a throne somewhere in Egypt. God's purpose for asking Moses to stoop was not evident at the time it all went down—perhaps it's the same in your situation. But rest assured that God is working in your life and circumstances the same way He was working in Moses'.

Forty years after Moses fled from Egypt, God sent him back there to deliver the children of Israel from bondage. By stooping just a little, he eventually received a huge promotion. Egypt's prince became Israel's deliverer—but somewhere in the middle he had to become Midian's shepherd so he could learn how to lead in a godly way.

Have you been asked to stoop lately? Have you been

removed from a position of leadership and influence you once had? Has God asked you to give up something you love so you can embrace something else?

Being in Two Places at Once

Unless you are standing on a state line somewhere, with one foot in one state and your other foot in another state, you cannot be in two places at once, no matter how hard you try.

When I was in high school I was a student leader within my high school youth group. A friend of mine was the junior high pastor at the time, and he called me up one day, needing a favor. He didn't have enough counselors to go to camp with his kids, so he asked me if I thought I could fill in for a weekend. I said yes, thinking it would only be a weekend-long commitment.

During that weekend God began to stir my heart for the junior high girls. They didn't have a lot of leaders, and the high school ministry was bursting with student leaders. When I first returned from the weekend, I began to pray about becoming involved in junior high ministry—but I didn't want to leave the position and status I held in my own youth group. I liked being known as a leader there.

So in the beginning I did both. I became a full-time leader with the junior high students, and I remained as a leader with the high school students. (Meanwhile, I was still in school and working part time.) It wasn't long before I burned out, trying to be in two places at once. The words of martyred missionary Jim Elliot now come to mind when I think of that time: "Wherever you are, be all there."[2] In exhaustion I prayed and asked the Lord what to do, and the answer was both clear and simple: "Step out of high school ministry and into junior high ministry."

At first, I didn't like God's answer. But I obeyed and stepped out of the ministry I was most comfortable in. I left the group of girls I could relate to most. I left my friends. And I poured my heart into ministering to the needs of the junior high girls around me. Two and a half years later, when I left junior high ministry to go to college, I saw that my time there had been fruitful. And I also saw that the high school ministry went along just fine without me. As much as I hated to admit it, the high school ministry did not *need* me.

Perhaps there is something in your life that you are involved with right now, and you feel as if God is asking you to release that particular thing and embrace something else—something uncomfortable or scary. Maybe you are trying to stand in two places at once. Let me encourage you to stoop while it is still your choice to do so. Nothing is worse than having God force us to stoop after we have stubbornly refused!

THE MASTER OF STOOPING

Mark 10:45 says, "For even the Son of Man did not come to be served, but to serve, and to give His life a ransom for many."

Jesus stooped—to the level of harlots, tax collectors, and beggars. He dined with thieves—in fact, He even invited a thief to be one of His twelve. He was the King of Kings in the flesh, and He came to be the servant of all. There can never be anyone who can stoop more than that. Many times we balk at the thought of spending time with those "beneath" us. Jesus never did. In fact, many times when in a crowd, those kinds of people came to Him and sought Him out. Real servants of Christ are approachable people. They do not have a celebrity or superstar mentality. They do not make you feel like you are inconveniencing them when you say hello or ask them for help.

> *Real servants of Christ are approachable people.*

Now that my own ministry is growing and I get invited to travel and speak, I sometimes find myself in the company of Christian authors and speakers who are very well known, even somewhat "famous." And it has been so refreshing for me to see how many of them are so normal. They are very real people who can have a normal conversation about something other than themselves. I watch them up close as their hearts break with people who approach them for prayer. And I am encouraged by the words of affirmation they share with me—someone who is just starting out in a realm of ministry in which they are well seasoned.

To me, these people are genuine portraits of Jesus because they are not afraid to stoop to a level beneath them and minister to those who will never write a book or take center stage at a weekend retreat. Stooping is the defining mark of an authentic servant. Just like Jesus, they are not afraid to get a little dirty or to be inconvenienced as they serve others—maybe even suffer some pain, as He did, in doing authentic ministry.

Perhaps the thought of stooping terrifies you. It's a thought that has always terrified me. But the truth is, we are never ready for the palaces until we have come to a place where we are comfortable in the desert. Moses could never have become Israel's deliverer without first becoming Midian's shepherd.

God needs to teach His leaders how to lead by first teaching them how to serve. Many times those they are called to serve are radically different from them. Sometimes the places they are called to serve are far from home and seem foreign. But that does not diminish the call and it should not affect our answer.

So let me ask you, where are you called to serve? How is God asking you to stoop right now? Why aren't you doing it?

FOR FURTHER THOUGHT:

1. How is God asking you to stoop right now?

2. What is something that you are scared to do that you feel God might call you to do?

3. Judging from Jesus' response to service in Mark 10:45, what should your attitude be like when God asks you to do something you don't want to do?

4. What are some examples from your past when God asked you to stoop? What happened as a result?

5. Who are some other biblical examples (besides Moses and Jesus) asked by God to stoop in order to be of service to His kingdom?

TAKING THE CHALLENGE:

Ask the Lord how He would have you to stoop this week. Maybe it's by talking to someone at school you wouldn't normally talk to. Perhaps it's signing up for a mission trip with less than first-class accommodations, or volunteering at a soup kitchen in your own town. However God shows you to stoop, put it into practice and actually do it this week.

Notes

1. Craig Dunham and Doug Serven, *TwentySomeone* (Denver, CO: Waterbrook Press, 2003), 181.
2. Elisabeth Elliot, *Passion and Purity* (Grand Rapids, MI: Fleming H. Revell, 1984), 80.

5

Out of the Box and Onto the Battlefield

When I was a freshman in college, Student Underground came to the Biola University campus and facilitated their Persecuted Church simulation. Students who wanted to participate—and high school students from surrounding youth groups—were invited to spend a Friday night learning about what thousands of persecuted Christians around the world experience regularly just for worshiping God.

The simulation was intense. So much so that I chose not to go through it as a participant. I opted instead to help with running it, and they made me a member of the "secret police." Each participant was assigned a classroom that represented their church, and another location that represented their home. As they passed back and forth between the locations throughout the night, the secret police jumped out and questioned them. If they gave away the fact that they were Christians, they were immediately taken to "interrogation rooms," where their faith would be put to the test.

Granted, it was a simulation, but the only instructions given to us in the "secret police" meeting were that we could not injure the participants. We could embarrass or scare them as much as possible so that they would have at least a somewhat accurate picture of what persecuted Christians experience.

I worked in one of the "interrogation rooms" with a guy named Tim. We had the lights off, the windows covered, and we had to try to coerce participants into reading statements such as, "God is dead." Some cried. Others laughed because they weren't taking it seriously. Many were shaking with fear by the time they actually made it to our room.

At one point, when I opened the door to let another participant in, there was a row of eight to ten of them on their knees in the mud with their hands on their heads. Some people said the simulation went too far. But those who ran it claimed that it gave us only a small glimpse of what many Christians endure on a daily basis.

That night, when I returned to my dorm room, I felt guilty. My heart hurt for those who had denied their faith in a pretend situation. Many had done it simply to end the "torture," and I honestly wondered if I would have done the same. The persecuted church was such a foreign concept to me up until that night. I just could not wrap my mind around the reality of being harassed, beaten, and maybe even killed just for going to church. Even with the consequences, many Christians around the world serve the Lord faithfully under such circumstances.

I know part of the purpose that night was to increase my

global awareness as a Christian. But my mind was stuck somewhere else, somewhere closer to home. Every time I closed my eyes that night I saw her face. She had long blond hair to her elbows and a gorgeous smile. I had seen her picture on television several years before. Only two months older than me at the time, she looked as if she could have been one of my friends. She was a typical teenager and her name was Cassie Bernall.

She said "Yes"

On April 20, 1999, she walked into the library at Columbine High School, as she had done many times before. She had English that period and one thing, and one thing only, was on her mind: Macbeth. Cassie was one of those students who always managed to get her work done—even if sometimes she finished it at the last minute. But this particular assignment was never completed. Before the period was over, two of Cassie's fellow students burst into the library with guns, seeking to destroy anyone and everyone they came across. Cassie, an outspoken Christian, was one they saw and sought out.

"Do you believe in God?" The question did not even hang in the air for a full minute before Cassie answered, although I'm sure it seemed as if the pause lasted an hour.

"Yes." With one small word Cassie's life was over.

In her bestselling book, *She Said Yes,* Cassie's mom, Misty, paints a painfully honest portrait of Cassie. She was not someone who had it all figured out. There were points in her life where she faltered. There were moments when she distanced herself from God for the sake of this world. But Cassie made a turnaround and a firm commitment to the Lord. Later, in a moment when it really mattered, she gave God all she had.

The night before she died she wrote a letter to her friend Amanda and gave it to her at school the next morning. At the bottom were the words: "P. S. Honestly, I want to live completely for God. It's hard and scary, but totally worth it."[1]

Her story brings new meaning to the word *persecution*. Right here, in middle-class America, a beautiful seventeen-year-old girl lost her life because of her faith. Her courage stirs a passion in each of us that makes us hope we would do the same if it were asked of us.

THE DIFFERENCE BETWEEN LIFE AND DEATH

Why is it that so many of us who hope that we would one day have the courage to die for Christ cannot seem to find the courage to really live for Him? The subtitle of this book says it all. Serving means learning to find your life by giving it away. That does not always mean dying a martyr's death like it did in Cassie's case. Sometimes it simply means caring more about others than you do about yourself. It may mean giving up a fun summer afternoon with friends because you were already committed to teaching a Vacation Bible School class at your church. It might mean giving up an entire weekend to baby-sit for free or serve food in a homeless shelter. As all genuine servants know,

BEING A GIRL WHO SERVES

at one point or another, serving God and serving others will cost you in some way.

Somehow our thinking is off, and we consider *living* for Christ more costly than *dying* for Him. When we live for Him, actively serving Him and taking a stand for what is right, we have to endure the rejection and ridicule of people we so desperately want to please and impress. Enduring a dirty look and a snide remark because of our faith is as bad as it's gotten for most of us.

> *We consider living for Christ more costly than dying for Him.*

"Are you a Christian?" The question pops up everywhere, from school to work and even when we are out having fun with our friends.

"Oh, um, well, my family goes to church," we answer, acting as if it's not really something we *want* to do, but rather something we *have* to do.

"Are you religious?" This question is usually asked in a rude tone.

"Well, sorta." We shrug and move on.

Perhaps you are more assertive than that. Maybe you stand up for your faith. If given the opportunity, like Cassie Bernall, you would stand up and do the right thing too. If so, good for you. But when we are honest, I think we would all admit we could afford to work on this area just a little bit more.

Hebrews 13:12–16 says, "Therefore Jesus also, that He might sanctify the people through His own blood, suffered outside the gate. Hence, let us go out to Him outside the camp, bearing His reproach. For here we do not have a lasting city, but we are seeking the city which is to come."

I love the last part of that passage: *We are seeking the city which is to come.* As teenagers we are most often caught up in the here and now. And why not? The here and now is fun! We're supposed to be having the time of our lives, right? Yes, but we need to look at what that really means for us as Christians.

For those of us who faithfully seek to serve God, having the time of our lives means seeking the kingdom that is to come. It means making our lives count for something. It means living for something that will live longer than we ever will. Simply put, it means leaving a legacy—and not just any legacy but a legacy worth following.

It means taking the opportunity to lead others to the Lord—and to share our faith with them—even when it is scary or difficult. Sharing our faith is not always an easy task, especially when we share with those who are desperately in need of a Savior but just don't want to admit their need or even the existence of Him. But even in situations like that, we are still called to share our faith and serve God by sharing the good news with others.

Most of us serve God in ways that are comfortable, in ways we are familiar with, in ways that are carefree, light-hearted, and fun. But some tasks require something more from us. Some service opportunities call us to get our hands dirty and get blood on our clothes because they walk us right into the midst of the greatest war that's ever been fought.

Sometimes being a servant means nothing more—and nothing less—than standing up for your faith in a situation where loving God is unpopular. It means refusing to be seen at parties where drinking, smoking, and sleeping around are going on. It means choosing to be single instead of dating or "hooking up with" that really hot unsaved guy who makes all of the girls in your class drool. It means waking up early for prayer and quiet time with the Lord even though you were up late studying for your algebra test.

Many times being a girl who serves means doing things that are uncomfortable and taking risks. First Corinthians 10:24 talks about always seeking the good of our neighbors, which we all know can be difficult to do at times. But look at it like this: If you woke up in the middle of the night and saw flames shooting out of your neighbor's second-story window, you would do something about it, right? You would call 9-1-1 or try to douse the house with your yard hose or some-thing. But one thing I am almost certain you wouldn't do is go and jump in your car and speed off thinking, *That's their problem, they can deal with it,* without doing anything to help.

In a crisis, it is more than likely that serving your neighbor would be at the forefront of your mind. So why is it that the crisis of someone's lack of salvation doesn't call us to action like that? Second Timothy 4:2 tells us to be ready "in season and out of season" to share our faith. Farther down, in verse 5, Paul tells us to "endure hardship, do the work of an evangelist, fulfill your ministry." Those are our marching orders— we don't have any excuse not to carry them out. But oftentimes we refuse to obey His clear commands.

FROM THE BOX TO THE BATTLEFIELD

So many times we Christians live life like a Jack-in-the-box. We have our personal comfort zone, with areas we are at ease serving in and things that are familiar to us. We don't "pop" out of our boxes very often. And we most certainly never *live* outside of our boxes. But the truth is, as Christians, we were not made to live in boxes. We were made to live on the battlefield.

When we live in boxes we are surrounded by walls—walls we have built to protect ourselves. If we try to grow within the confines of these walls we become dwarfed versions of what God designed us to be. He wants us to grow *outside* of the confines of our walls. He wants us to serve Him in areas beyond the borders of any of our boxes. He wants us to serve Him on the front lines of the battlefield.

One high school girl I know gave up a good portion of her summer (and time with her new boyfriend, whom she had waited an entire year to be able to date) and served God by volunteering at a camp for abused and troubled children. She saw a need, and her heart was tugged to fill it even though it would cost her some fun.

Another girl I know decided to spend an entire summer in Belize—away from her friends and family—serving with a missionary family there. These girls didn't spend their summers in youth group *learning about* serving others. They spent their summers *doing it.* They got out of their boxes and onto the battlefield.

When we seek to serve God and it costs us something—when we get out of our boxes—we grow. And God delights in watching us grow. He takes joy in seeing us become more and more like Him. When we stand for what is right in a world

God delights in watching us grow.

that is living for everything wrong, God rejoices in who we are becoming.

In most of our lives all-out persecution will only be something we will read about in books or see on TV. But each of us will have our fair share of smaller persecutions. There will be moments when serving God will cost us popularity, friendships, maybe even comfort and stability. But when you find yourself weeping into a tearstained pillow, think for just a moment about what true persecution is. Pray for those who endure it. Thank God that your persecutions are on a smaller scale.

One thing I would strongly encourage any girl to do is to go on a mission trip of some kind. You can go to Africa, Asia, South America, or Eastern Europe. You can go to an orphanage in Mexico or a homeless shelter in your own city. You can even help at a group home around the corner from where you live. It doesn't matter where you go as long as you break out of your box for a few moments. As Christians, we often become comfortable with the idea of serving God by serving other Christians. We opt for opportunities teaching Sunday school, teaching a Bible study, or greeting people as they come in the door.

These are great opportunities. I taught a girls' Bible study at my church and I loved it. I only stopped because I got married and moved away. Although opportunities like that do involve us in the fight, they don't put us on the *front lines*. There will always be a need for great Sunday school teachers and Bible study leaders, and I'm not saying that we aren't serving God by filling these positions. But we also need to be aware that there is a very desperate need for Christians to go out and minister to those who do not know Christ. Here is where you will encounter the fierce battle of the front lines as you war for the souls of people—that they might be delivered from the kingdom of darkness into the kingdom of light.

It's great to have ministries within the church that are focused on helping other Christians grow, but we cannot be completely self-contained, spending time *only* with other

Christians. It may feel safe, but it's more like a cocoon that binds us up in ourselves, making us unable to reach out like God intended.

It's time that we broke out of our boxes. If we don't tell the world just how great a salvation we have, they will never know. Matthew 28:19 tells us to make disciples of all the nations—not just to make disciples within the church. That does not necessarily mean we need to stand on wooden crates and start preaching from the street corners. But we at least should be making attempts at friendship evangelism (befriending non-Christians so that we can share our faith with them as our friendship grows).

At times in my life I have had tons of exposure to non-Christians (like when I was attending public school). But there have also been times when my exposure to the unsaved has been limited due to my own unwillingness to get out of the box.

It is in those moments when I am only surrounded by other Christians that I feel as if I am somehow missing my purpose. Yes, it is vitally important to help others grow in their walk with the Lord, but it is even more important for us to take time to help lead those to Christ who do not even know Him. They are the ones who so desperately need His saving grace.

The Battlefield as a Mission Field

Oftentimes we act as if it is hard to find people to witness to, people with whom we can share our faith. But in all honesty they are probably closer than we think. We may even encounter them every day—or at least on a regular basis. Most of us probably have some unsaved relatives, neighbors, or friends of friends that we could greatly impact for God's glory if we would only take the time. We don't need to preach at people. They need to be loved into the kingdom—and we are just the people God has called to do it.

So many times the people around us are on their way to hell, yet we are afraid they will make fun of us if they know we go to church on Sunday because we *want* to. Recently, I was convicted in a conversation I was having with some friends about how hard it is to relate to non-Christian family members.

I have many non-Christian aunts, uncles, and cousins, and now that I have married into my husband's family I have even more. Yet when I see these people several times each year, I usually stick with conversations that are comfortable. I avoid talking about my faith or my ministry. I don't take a risk because I don't want to argue or be ridiculed or backed into a corner in the middle of Thanksgiving dinner.

When someone I know passed away a few years ago, I remember being so grieved by not knowing whether or not she ever came to Christ. But I could remember several memorable conversations I had with her about my own faith and her need for a Savior. I did not have to wrestle with guilt because I knew I had done my part. Our battlefield is our mission field. The souls of those around us are definitely worth fighting for.

Most of us agree that we want to spend our lives for a worthy cause. Yet so many times we give our attention and our time to things that are far less than worthy. Make it your goal to have at least one honest conversation about your faith with those you love. You don't have to preach at them. Simply let them know what you believe and why.

> *The souls of those around us are definitely worth fighting for.*

When I was in high school, I had a friend who was raised in the Hindu faith. We met our junior year and since both of us were only children, we had a common bond right away. We had a lot of classes together, and pretty soon we started to hang out outside of school too. One night, during our senior year, she was over at my house watching movies and spending the night. Something in one of the movies we watched launched us into a conversation about life, faith, and what we believed about God and heaven.

Very gently, I shared about my belief in the need for a Savior. As I began to talk about Jesus Christ and the gospel message, my friend's brow wrinkled.

"Who is Jesus?" Her question was honest. She knew He was a "religious leader" but had never heard about His dying on the cross. I got my Bible and shared with her for what seemed like hours.

"I believe what you are saying is true," she said, "because of the way you live your life and how passionate you are when you talk about it. But I'm not there yet. I would rather have some more fun and party just a little more before giving it all up."

We kept in touch until somewhere in the middle of college—when life got busy and e-mail addresses and phone numbers changed. I took a risk sharing with my friend that night. She was very popular and had a lot of pull on campus. Boldly, though, I shared *with* her without preaching *at* her.

Most times she thoughtfully listened, although sometimes she would tease me or pressure me when we were in big crowds. I took her occasional insults in stride, standing for the truth no matter the cost. Once it cost me a spot on the Homecoming Queen ballot. And although it mattered to me then, it doesn't now. I can look back on that time in my life and know that I stood for what was right, sharing the Gospel with boldness.

In the end, each of us only gets one life. What we choose to do with it is up to us. We can either serve God in the safe confines of the church, or we can serve Him on the front lines of places few Christians dare to go. Although both forms of ministry have their place, one is more challenging than the other. One is riskier than the other. Sometimes it's the one that prepares us for the other. But the bottom line is that we should always be serving Him somewhere—and everywhere.

Cassie Bernall knew the God she loved and served very well. When she was put on the front lines, she knew the answer to the question she was asked because she had asked it of herself many times. "Do you believe in God?" She said yes. And she lived yes too. I pray that if asked, each of us would do the same.

FOR FURTHER THOUGHT:

1. What is your "box"? What are the walls you put up to protect yourself from ridicule and rejection?

2. What do you see as your battle/mission field?

3. What are some ways you can get out of your box and onto the battlefield, to stand up for your faith in an active setting?

4. Which do you think is harder: living for Jesus or dying for Him? Why?

5. What is the difference between *sharing with* someone and *preaching at* someone? Which is more effective?

TAKING THE CHALLENGE:

Find one person you can share your faith with this week. Be creative and relational in your approach—don't preach at them. Be bold yet tactful. Get out of your box and onto the battlefield!

Notes

1. Misty Bernall, *She Said Yes* (Farmington, PA: The Plough Publishing Group, 1999).

6

Busier Isn't Always Better

All forty of us were sitting in a large circle in the upper room at the retreat center in Mexico. We were undergoing some intense training before being sent out as mission-trip leaders. Getting ready to have a time of worship and a short Bible study on leadership and servanthood, we were all trying to make ourselves comfortable in accommodations that were anything but. Most of us stretched and fidgeted, trying to relax. We were cold and the hard cement floors only made it worse. "Maggie" (not her real name) was over at the Communion table fussing with things, trying to get everything ready.

"Let's pray before we begin," our professor, Murray, said in a tired yet steady voice. Most of us bowed our heads and closed our eyes. But Murray did not pray. A loud clatter interrupted our thoughts. We all looked toward Maggie.

"Maggie—Martha—get over here!" Murray called out.

"But I—" she began, but Murray cut her off.

"We can take care of all of that later," he said patiently as he looked toward the Communion table. "Why don't you come over here and join us as we pray?" I felt for Maggie in that moment. She was trying so hard to ready everything for the rest of us. A faithful servant, and someone who was always willing to roll up her sleeves, Maggie was the type of person you would want on your team.

She was obviously embarrassed by the negative attention—I could tell by the red circles forming on her cheeks as she took her seat next to the rest of us.

"Sorry," she mumbled, looking down. As Murray prayed and went on talking about the importance of servant leadership, my mind wandered back to Maggie, and then back even further to Martha and her sister Mary.

THE DISTRACTED SERVANT

Luke 10:38–42 gives the account of two sisters—both with servants' hearts but with two very different ideas of service. Martha was very much like my friend Maggie—and that's why Murray referred to Maggie as "Martha."

Martha in the Bible was a busy homemaker. She was probably a Martha Stewart type in her day, with freshly baked cookies on the counter and perfectly arranged fresh-cut flowers on every table in the house.

When she heard Jesus was coming, Martha no doubt made sure the house was immaculate, and that the finest foods and drinks available were brought in. Verse 40 tells us Martha was *distracted* with her preparations for Jesus' visit. It's hard to imagine an attitude of service being referred to as a distraction.

How many times in our own lives do we get distracted while serving the Lord? Notice, I did not say distracted *from* serving the Lord but rather distracted *while* serving the Lord. Martha's biggest problem was that she paid more attention to the household details than she did to Jesus. It probably happened so fast that she didn't even realize it.

Often, it's the same in our lives. Recently a friend of mine was committed to teaching a Bible study, but he didn't set aside any time to study. Instead, he got caught up in doing other things—cleaning the house, balancing his checkbook, and other small tasks like that. When I asked him what he was going to do about it, he said he was going to forgo his quiet time for the next two mornings and study then. How quickly we can become like Martha without even realizing it!

We justify our distractions because we are doing something *for* the Lord, so it doesn't make it seem so bad that we are not spending time *with* Him. And how many times do we get distracted from anything related to the Lord at all? We wake up late, we furiously get ready for school as fast as we can, and on our way out the door we casually look at our Bible—which has gone unopened all morning—and without another thought we leave for the day. Why is it that when other things come up, our time with the Lord is the first thing to go?

In college one of my friends admitted she spent more time perfectly applying her mascara than she did reading her Bible in the mornings. Most of us can relate—we care more about what we look like than we do about the spiritual state of our hearts.

Time spent with Jesus is vital to servants of God. If we are not spending time in God's Word and in prayer, nothing else matters. I'm sure Jesus appreciated Martha's efforts on the day He came to visit her in her home. But there was something He appreciated even more: Mary's attitude of service.

Worried and Bothered by Many Things

Martha got frustrated at her sister Mary for not helping her with meal preparations. After Jesus arrived in their home, Martha even went so far as to ask Him to put Mary in her place! Now there's a disgruntled servant for you. She had too much to do and she tried to demand that someone else help her. But notice Jesus' response to Martha the Super Servant.

Time spent with Jesus is vital to servants of God.

"Martha, Martha," He says in verse 41, "you are worried and bothered about so many things; but only a few things are necessary, really only one, for Mary has chosen the good part, which shall not be taken away from her."

Imagine being Martha in that moment. Already worried and bothered by many things, I'm sure Jesus' response became another thing to bother and perplex her. Didn't He see how hard she had worked to make every detail right for His visit? Why didn't He notice her good deeds and commend her, rather than defend Mary (the slacker)? Here she was, slaving away with the preparations, and there Mary was getting all of the attention.

Don't you just hate that? You are already worried and

bothered about the details in the situations surrounding you. You are trying your hardest to make sure everything goes right. You are carrying your own weight—and everyone else's. And then someone else comes along, doing nothing really, and *she* gets all of the attention and praise. Had I been Martha that day, I'm sure I would have burst into tears at the sound of Jesus' words and simply let dinner burn on the stove.

His words to her that day could be interpreted as hurtful if they are misunderstood. For those of us like Martha—and my friend Maggie—who are so accustomed to doing things for the Lord (and everyone else), it's hard to understand why *doing something* isn't always the best thing.

When someone tells us that there is something better that we could be doing, we have a tendency to freak out because we misunderstand what they are saying. We interpret it to mean that we are not doing enough, when really all they meant is that we are doing too much or that we are doing the wrong thing entirely or at the wrong time.

Burned Out on Service

During my last year and a half of college I started a girls' Bible study in my apartment. My last semester I got to a place where I felt overloaded. Although we planned to take turns teaching the girls' Bible study, I always ended up teaching a lot of the time. When we got ready to resume after our summer break, I sat the girls down and told them that I would not be teaching at all for my final semester. The most I was able to do was open my apartment and attend.

I was burned out on service, I was overloaded with school-work, and I came home from work every day feeling as if I had accomplished nothing because I wasn't working enough hours to really do my job well. To top it all off, I was trying to squeeze interviews with several radio stations for my first book in between my classes! Adding one more thing to my plate would have sent me into overload and I would never have made it to graduation.

The hardest part for me, though, was that no one under-stood why I was opting not to teach my final semester. I was the one who *started* the Bible study, and somewhere along the line I became the unofficial leader. Many of the girls privately—and not so privately—pulled me aside in the days and months that followed to ask me if I was slipping in my walk. We were a Bible study full of Marthas, and no one could understand my desire to simply sit at Jesus' feet like Mary.

I chose not to defend my actions. Instead, I just reassured them I wasn't slipping in my walk and then moved on in the conversation. When they looked at me to lead a discussion I sat quietly until someone else stepped up to the plate. It was one of the hardest things I ever did because I am a natural leader. I was dying to jump into the conversation and share all of my insights or draw others in the group out of their shells. Many of the details of Bible study seemed to be falling apart because I wasn't worrying about them.

But I can honestly tell you that it turned out to be a great experience. Through it I learned what Jesus meant by choosing the "good part" during that time in my life. There was freedom that came from not trying to lead where I didn't *need* to lead and from not trying to hold everyone and everything together, making sure Bible study went perfectly each week. I was no longer distracted by all those details. For the first time ever I could focus on the text we were discussing and sit back and fellowship with other girls who attended.

It's amazing how much peace I experienced when I wasn't worried about cleaning the kitchen after our weekly potluck. In fact, I think it was the first time I actually realized we were all gathered together *to study God's Word*. Not surprisingly, another Martha popped up in the group and became the one to fuss and fix everything around us. But I looked at her and saw that her peace was gone because of it. For the first time in a long time I had chosen the good part, and the joy in my expression showed it.

The world is full of Marthas. We don't need more. Fact is, we could afford to have a few less. Perhaps you, too, are a natural leader. Maybe you fuss at and fix everything in everyone's life around you. Maybe being the busy servant gives you a feeling of self worth and accomplishment. Maybe the thought of choosing the "good part" terrifies you. Perhaps you are afraid if you take time to sit at Jesus' feet He might say something to you that you wouldn't like. But don't let your fears and insecurities keep you from discovering the joy of the "good part"—it's truly the best way to serve Christ!

A DIFFERENT KIND OF SERVICE

Jesus' words in verse 41 really strike me. "... only a few things are necessary, really only one." I don't know how many things I think are necessary in life. But I can tell you my answer certainly isn't *one*. My guess is that you feel the same way. But those words came straight from Jesus himself, and He does not lie. That means God is not looking for us to do everything we possibly can do. We don't have to lead everyone on our school campus to Christ, earn a 4.0 GPA, be an all-around athlete, and sing on our youth group worship team.

Before any servant can serve, she must sit.

Even if we only did one of those things we would still be missing the point. Before any servant can serve, she must sit. She must sit at the feet of Jesus and simply bask in His presence. She must take joy in her relationship with Him. She must stop striving, fighting, leading, fussing, and fixing for a moment and simply just *be*. The good part is a different kind of service. It's simply taking time for no one and nothing else but Jesus. Forget about the details and remember Jesus.

Just the other morning I woke up overloaded by all that was on my to-do list. I was doing too much. As Beth Moore said in one of her video Bible studies, "I put fifteen things where only one belongs." So I did something completely uncharacteristic of me. I put my long list aside and spent some extra time with Jesus that morning. I knew that being my typical Martha self was not going to work that time. The good part was absolutely necessary if I was going to make it through my day.

Later on, I was able to go through my day with increased energy and accomplish everything I had on my list because I had renewed my strength by taking some time to sit at the feet of Jesus. On days when it seems like you may not have a moment to spare, setting extra time aside to meet with Christ can and will work wonders.

Now, that does not give us an excuse to be lazy and not get out there and serve the Lord at all. But it does mean that we should make sure we are spending plenty of time with God before rushing out to serve Him. We all need to take advantage of moments where everything on our lists can wait—and we need to take time just to sit at the feet of Jesus.

So leave the dishes piled in the sink and ignore the ringing phone for a moment. Let the other Marthas of this world tend to the trillions of menial tasks. Come into the other room for a while, join Mary on the floor at Jesus' feet, and bask in the good part, the other side of service.

FOR FURTHER THOUGHT:

1. When was the last time you experienced the good part in your life?

2. What is it about the good part that scares or intimidates you?

3. What are some things that distract you from serving the Lord?

4. Are you more prone to be a Mary or a Martha? How so?

5. What do you think Jesus meant when He said Mary had chosen the "good part"?

TAKING THE CHALLENGE:

Forgo something you normally do this week (homework probably isn't a good choice) and simply sit at the feet of Jesus. Spend time in His presence. Communicate with the Lord through prayer and reading His Word. Bask in the good part.

7

An Invitation to the Table

Life was hard for him. Getting around was difficult because he walked with a limp, and he was very slow. The clicking of his cane could be heard in the distance as he approached. I'm sure he wondered why the king had summoned him. Fear most likely gnawed at his heart as he approached the throne that had once belonged to his own family. Although he had been born into royalty, there was nothing regal about Mephibosheth. He was heir to a conquered regime. His lot in life was to live in obscurity outside of Jerusalem, as far from the palace walls as he could get.

His life would have continued on in a like manner had David—God's faithful servant and Israel's reigning king—not sought an opportunity to serve someone who did not deserve it. Notice, David *sought* an opportunity to serve someone else. David did not pass poor, crippled Mephibosheth begging for money on the city streets and just throw him some change. No, he went looking for someone like him to serve—and David was a king!

How often, in our own lives, do we actually *look* for people to serve? How many times do we blow by the people we can see with needs (people we don't have to seek out) without stopping?

Second Samuel 9 gives us a glimpse into what the heart of a true servant looks like. Right in the middle of what some would consider the prime of David's reign, he seeks out anyone remaining from the house of Saul so that he might show kindness to them. This was unusual because most kings wanted all members of a previous king's family dead so they would never pose a threat to his kingdom. David, though, did not gain his throne through violence, and he wouldn't attempt to keep it by violence either.

When informed that there is one son of Jonathan still alive, David is elated and sends for him immediately. David and Jonathan had shared a deep and true friendship. Perhaps David's mind even raced back to the day recorded in 1 Samuel 20:42 when David and Jonathan made a covenant to each other saying, " 'The Lord will be between me and you, and between my descendants and your descendants forever.' "

Second Samuel 4:4 tells us that immediately following Jonathan's death, Mephibosheth was dropped by his nurse, who was trying to run to safety in haste. This accident claimed his right to walk in the same moment his father's (and grandfather's) death forfeited his right to the throne. Mephibosheth was unfortunate. He was probably the type of man people turned away from when they passed him by.

THREE IMPORTANT PARTS OF SERVING WELL

But David did not turn away. When Mephibosheth came and fell on his face at David's feet, David assured him he was brought to the kingdom for good and not for evil. "Mephibosheth . . . do not fear, for I will surely show kindness to you for the sake of your father Jonathan, and will restore to you all the land of your grandfather Saul; and you shall eat at my table regularly" (2 Samuel 9:6–7). In David's words to Mephibosheth we find three things a servant of God should do when serving someone else.

The Name Game

David called him by name. There is just something about hearing the sound of your own name. Even when you are in a crowded mall or in the hallway during passing period at school, your head automatically turns at the sound of your own name— even if someone is calling out to someone else who shares the same first name as you. We like people to use our names because it gives us a sense of worth.

In college, I became the type of person who writes her name on everything. If I get a new DVD I write my last name on it before putting it on the shelf so that if it is borrowed—or comes up missing—it will be easier to spot amongst someone else's things. A girl who lived on my floor my sophomore year took this whole name thing so far that she wrote her name on the tags inside her clothes! That way if she loaned them out she had a better chance of getting them back.

Names are important. And we should use them as much as possible with the people whom we serve. Once I was teaching a workshop at a very large event. I met so many women that I could never remember all of their names if I tried. Most of the time I would forget their name the second they walked away. But on the last night of the weekend a woman approached me at my book table with tears in her eyes.

"You remembered my name."

I had met her earlier that afternoon, and oddly enough I remembered her name—so I used it when I greeted her. It stopped her in her tracks. "You remembered my name," she said in astonishment as the tears began to flow. She proceeded to tell me she felt unimportant when she came up the mountain for the retreat, but God had used the weekend to remind her that *He* called her by name. The fact that I also used her name when I greeted her was just another reminder of that fact.

It was a powerful moment for me. It taught me the importance of putting effort into learning people's names. Simply by smiling at someone as they pass you in the hall at school gives them *encouragement*. Saying hello and using their name as you do it gives them *value*. Jesus always affirmed those around Him, giving them a sense of self-worth. Gently and lovingly Jesus ascribed value to tax collectors, thieves, and prostitutes. He dined with them; He stopped and talked to them on city streets—right there in front of everyone.

He wasn't afraid to be associated with them. He wasn't too proud to know them by name. If He thought that even the lowest of the lowly deserved to be valued, imagine how much value He would ascribe to those you deem unimportant or unworthy in your own life.

David calls Mephibosheth by his name in this passage, treating him as a human being and not the "dead dog" Mephibosheth refers to himself as (v. 8). Instead of basking in Mephibosheth's humble state, and standing tall as a lord over Mephibosheth's broken life ("Sorry buddy, but *I'm* in the royal line now"), David takes a step down from the platform he has been placed on and he treats Mephibosheth as an equal, calling him by his name.

Haven't there been times in your life when you desperately wanted someone to know your name? When I was in high school there were several times I was caught off guard when a teacher I had years earlier saw me in the hallway and said hello to me—and they remembered my name. Having so many students per semester, it was common at my high school for them to forget the names of most of the students they encountered once a semester was through. When one would remember my name I would always feel special for the next week or so.

Names are a big part of who we are, whether they are first names, last names, or nicknames. For most of us, our names define who we are. Sometimes they even demonstrate the depth of relationship we have with others. My husband's name is Michael—but only those of us who are really close to him call him that. Everyone else calls him Mike. When we first began dating, I called him Mike because that is how he was introduced to me. As time went on, and we fell in love, he asked me to call him Michael, signifying the fact that he was inviting me into a deeper and closer relationship with him. Names are a very personal and intimate thing.

Think of it this way: If you met the president of the United States and he called you by your name, I'm sure you would feel a certain sense of importance over the fact that he knew your name, *and he used it*. When your name is used you are not just part of the crowd—you are instantly an individual with value and worth.

Who do you pass in the hall every day that you have never paid any attention to? Who do you have in your life that you can serve by simply ascribing value to them and learning their name?

Easy Does It

David also made a point to put Mephibosheth at ease in his presence. "Do not fear . . ." he said. How those words must have sounded like music to the ears of one who hobbled into the palace that day thinking he was going to be put to death! Although the Bible does not tell us the tone of David's voice that day, I'm sure it was gentle and kind. He most likely smiled when he looked at the son of his deceased friend Jonathan. Perhaps his heart was warmed as he saw a slight resemblance to Jonathan in Mephibosheth's face.

There was nothing intimidating about David's royalty once he spoke, because he replaced his kingship with friendship. He made himself real and vulnerable as he extended his hand to help someone he did not have to help. Just as much as Mephibosheth was Jonathan's son, he was also Saul's grandson, and Saul had never treated David right—not once. Had it been up to Saul, David would have been placed in his grave long ago.

David did not try to make Mephibosheth pay for the sins of those who came before him. He didn't try to take revenge on Saul by finishing off his family. If anything, David took the grace that had been extended to him by Jonathan, and he extended it to Mephibosheth tenfold.

How different things are in the lives of teenage girls. Those of us who ever receive the upper hand would rather die than surrender it. Stepping down from our pedestals is not really an option. We like power, prestige, and authority. When we feel as if we are better than someone else, we feel pretty good about ourselves.

Sometimes God's servants are elevated to positions of prestige, leadership, and authority. Some of us take our place on thrones or in spotlights like David did. But we should never look down on the Mephibosheths of this world. We should never make others uncomfortable in our presence just because we can. We, too, need to be like David and put others at ease in our presence.

Recently, I met a couple who lives in a mobile home in a rough little town. At one point in their lives they had been very wealthy. But they felt God telling them to sell their precious BMWs and live among people who had never seen anything nicer than the junkyard's finest car. On a recent visit with this couple, we were in their living room talking when a neighbor came over and walked right inside their front door without knocking. He said hello and headed straight to the kitchen and helped himself to something to eat.

When this couple moved in, they let the neighbors know they had an open-door policy. People could come in and grab something to eat, shower, or even crash for the night if they needed to. And many of them did. They walked into this home as if it were their own because this couple put them at ease. They made people feel welcome and comfortable.

Because of this they were able to serve the people—and reach the people—in ways far greater than they had ever imagined when they first moved to the run-down neighborhood. The neighbors accepted them, even though they were different, because they had accepted their neighbors as they were first.

Once I was invited to breakfast by one of my favorite authors of all time. She was my role model, and a big part of the reason why I wanted to write books. She captured all I wanted to accomplish with my own writing career. I remember being so nervous sitting at that breakfast table in the crowded restaurant on the day I first met her in person. In an attempt to calm my nerves I reached for the nearest water glass, not realizing it was hers! I was so embarrassed once I realized it, but she never gave me a reason to be. She put me at ease immediately and we managed to have a fun and lighthearted breakfast.

We have since become friends. We talk on the phone and exchange e-mails every now and then, and we have spent time together on other occasions. That all happened because someone with superstar status made it a point to put an average girl like me at ease. She set an example we should all follow.

The Gift That Keeps on Giving

More than anything else David gave Mephibosheth that day, he gave him a place of belonging. David went above and beyond the call of duty when it came to generosity. "[I] will restore to you all the land of your grandfather Saul; and you shall eat at my table regularly," he said to Mephibosheth in verse seven. He invited the ousted prince to move back to the city of his heritage and into the place where his father and his grandfather once lived.

In a sense, he gave his birthright back to him. He let him come home. Any of us who have been away from home—even on a short vacation or mission trip—know how good it

He let him come home.

feels to be back home. When I moved home from college for my first summer vacation, it was refreshing to be back in my parents' house. It was such a relief to be back somewhere I was comfortable—somewhere that I could just be me.

I'm sure, in a much greater sense, Mephibosheth felt the same way. The second half of 2 Samuel 9:11 says, "So Mephibosheth ate at David's table as one of the king's sons." Not only did David give Mephibosheth a place to eat, but he treated him like the prince he was born to be. He gave him not only a place of belonging, but a place of *honor*. He gave him a permanent invitation to the king's table. Every night there was a seat with his name on it.

When I was in college I went on a mission trip with a bunch of other students whom I didn't know—aside from one girl who was a childhood friend of mine. Everyone else in the group was tight-knit. They got along great and had years of history and friendship with each other. But they never once made me feel like an outsider. They didn't form a clique and push me out of it. Instead, they welcomed me into their circle like I had always belonged. Because of that I had one of the most fun and refreshing summers of my entire life.

Most of us, though, are more concerned with our own seat at the table. We are too caught up in whether or not we are being given a place of honor to notice someone else's need. There are people in each of our lives that we could be serving. We just don't bother. We take a cursory glance around our school, our youth group, and our community and we claim that everything that needs to be done is being done. "There's no one left to serve," we say. And then we go on with our self-centered lives.

Unlike David, we don't *look* for opportunities to serve other people. We may take opportunities that come our way, but we never go out of our way. The world around us tells us that no one else (besides us) really matters, and unfortunately a lot of us live that way. But we can change the way we do things—it's not too late.

We can look for opportunities to serve others like David did. We can learn the names of those around us whom we haven't taken the time to notice before, and affirm them and give them value. We can put those who are insecure or uncomfortable at ease in our presence and we can always, always save someone else a seat—whether it's at our lunch table, on the school bus, or in our circle of friends.

But one of the greatest acts of service we can bestow on someone else is to give them a place of belonging and a sense of self-worth. Look for those who wander your school halls or work in the stores you shop at all the time. Look for the people you have never noticed or seen before. Ask God to direct you to someone you can simply be nice to and encourage. Make eye contact with them; offer them a warm smile and a simple hello. Extend your hand, learn their name—and invite them to come and join you at the Master's table.

The story of David and Mephibosheth is just a glimpse of the love and attitude of service and self-sacrifice exemplified in the Gospel. We were like Mephibosheth—broken, on the outskirts of heaven with nowhere to call home. And Christ came and rescued us—calling us by name, putting us at ease, and inviting us to take a permanent place at His table. We too have been redeemed and restored, just like Mephibosheth.

Because of this our hearts should burn with compassion as we set out to seek and serve those around us. The meal has been prepared, the fine china has been set out, and the moment has come. Who are you going to invite to *your* table right now?

FOR FURTHER THOUGHT:

1. How was David's kindness toward Mephibosheth an act of service? Was he serving God too through this action, or just Mephibosheth? How so?

2. Who are the people in your life that you need to look harder for and seek out?

3. What are some ways you can extend kindness to people in your life and "invite them to the table"?

4. In what ways have you seen God treat you the way David treated Mephibosheth?

5. What excuses do you use so that you do not have to go out of your way to serve others? What is wrong with those excuses?

TAKING THE CHALLENGE:

Find someone you see all the time yet do not know. Ask them their name and invite them to share their story. Put them at ease in your presence. Invite them into your life. And when your initial conversation is over, make sure you don't blow them off or forget about them. Make a new friend.

BEING A GIRL WHO SERVES

8

A Simple Sack Lunch

In the fall of 2004 I taught a weekly junior high girls' Bible study and a weekly high school girls' Bible study. Our combined attendance was close to fifty or sixty girls each week. When we first began meeting, we decided that it was going to be our goal to sponsor two needy families for Christmas (one family for each group).

On Tuesday nights I would set out a hot-pink piggy bank for the high school girls, and on Sunday nights I would set out another one for the junior high girls. Each week the girls would give a little of their extra money they made while baby-sitting or at their after-school jobs. Some would even give something out of their allowance.

Week after week girls would come to me asking for the pigs because they had money to add to them. One week a junior higher I know came with four Ziplock baggies full of loose change! At the end of our ten-week Bible study these girls had raised six hundred dollars for the two families.

I must have counted the money two or three times to make sure that my horrible math skills hadn't caused me to miscount our funds. Every time I added the numbers they came out the same—we had raised over and above our original goal.

Together the girls and I took advantage of holiday sales to make our money go further, and we were able to bless these families with much more than we had hoped or dreamed was possible. God took what little we had to give and made it something incredible in order to meet the needs of two families who were in tough financial situations.

After the first week of Bible study, when only a few dimes, nickels, and pennies (given by one of our leaders) rolled around in the belly of the hot-pink pig, it would have been easy to lose heart. But instead we committed to sponsoring our two families and stood back and watched God work.

I am always amazed at what God does when we simply give Him what little we have and allow Him to do whatever He wants with it. Matthew, Mark, Luke, and John were four very different men, and they wrote their four gospels in four different styles from four different perspectives. Occasionally we read the same story in two gospels, maybe three if we are lucky. But there is only one miracle that is recounted in all four gospels: the feeding of the five thousand.

Matthew 14:13–21, Mark 6:33–44, Luke 9:12–17, and John 6:1–14 all tell us about what God can do with just a little. Each of the gospel writers give attention to different details, but the story is very much the same no matter who tells it. It's an amazing account, no matter which perspective you read.

In this chapter, though, we are going to look primarily at John's account. There are three responses we need to take note of in this story: Philip's response to the situation, Andrew's response to the limited resources, and Jesus' response to both the situation and the waning faith of His disciples.

NOTHING TO GIVE

The first four verses tell us of the crowds that gathered to witness Jesus' miracles. Because they saw that Jesus had the power to supply their *wants*, they followed Him.[1] The disciples knew this and grew weary more quickly than Jesus did. In verse five Jesus lifts up His eyes, sees the need of the people, and turns to His disciple Philip, asking him where they can get bread for the people to eat. Verse six tells us He did this to test Philip, for Jesus knew He was about to perform a miracle.

Philip fails the test (as most of us would) and answers the Lord by saying, "Two hundred denarii worth of bread is not sufficient for them, for everyone to receive a little" (John 6:7).

In his commentary on the New Testament, theologian Adam Clarke says two hundred denarii is more than Jesus and all of His disciples were worth, based on their worldly goods. Perhaps Philip's response was even a little sarcastic or whiney. Most likely it was spoken out of exhaustion and exasperation.

In modern language it may have sounded something like this: "What do you mean, where can we get bread to feed all of these people? Even if we spent every last dime of all of us combined we would still not have enough for everyone to eat only a little, much less a lot." How often we are like Philip, trying to stand in God's way as He waits to unleash a miracle.

A few years ago I received an e-mail from a woman named Anna. She lived in East Los Angeles and attended a small church with no real youth program. She and her husband had a heart for youth, especially the troubled teens around them who would most likely give in to lifestyles of drugs, sex, and gang violence if no other alternative was provided for them. Anna wrote that God gave her a vision of hosting a "Passion for Purity" event for the girls in her neighborhood with me as the speaker.

She told me everyone in her office laughed at her when she e-mailed me and invited me to East L.A. to speak at a very small event funded out of her own not-so-deep pockets. They told her there was no way anyone would be willing to come out to their rough neighborhood, especially if they couldn't pay for a speaker. They figured most speakers were too busy with far bigger events to even give a second thought to their small, low-budget event.

But something about Anna's heart for the girls and her faith in God captivated me. After praying about it, I accepted her invitation without even hesitating. And on a crisp February afternoon, close to thirty girls attended the event that many had called impossible.

They came dressed as if they were attending a prom or a grand ball. Their hair was done and their makeup was flawless. The tables were draped in tablecloths, there were candles everywhere, and beautifully wrapped gifts sat at every girl's seat. Each girl received her very own purity ring that afternoon. It was an amazing event—more than even Anna could have ever imagined was possible.

Through several people who donated their time, money, and other items, God did a miracle in East Los Angeles, and the lives of many girls were radically changed as they came to understand that purity was possible for them. Anna stepped forward and gave her five barley loaves and two fish, and God fed a multitude. Unlike Philip, Anna passed her test, and we should aspire to do the same. She could have told God she didn't have enough money and that no one would ever come to her neighborhood. But she gave God what she had and watched Him work a miracle.

ALL WE'VE GOT IS STILL NOT ENOUGH

In John 6:8 Andrew comes to Jesus and informs Him that there is a little boy in the crowd who has five loaves of bread and two fish. He also looks at Jesus and asks, "But what are these for so many people?" How often have we all asked God that same question?

Several years ago I received an e-mail from a high school senior named Britany, who attended a large public school in a wealthy neighborhood. She knew she did not have a lot to offer the Lord, but she did have something: She could serve Him by opening her home for a weekly Bible study and inviting anyone and everyone at her school.

At first, things were slow in coming. Only a small trickle of students came. But by the time she graduated, Britany had close to two hundred students attending the Bible study she started in faith. Nearly sixty of them came to Christ. I met Britany the summer before she left for college, when I was in her home state of Georgia at a youth event. I'll never forget the wonder and amazement in her eyes as she told me of what God had done.

Things had become so much bigger—and had gone on for so much longer—than she could have ever imagined. She couldn't believe what God had done with her just because she was willing. What she felt that day was close to what the boy with the five barley loaves and two fish must have felt on the afternoon he watched Jesus feed a multitude with his simple lunch.

God does not ask us for everything in existence—He knows we don't have that. He simply asks us for *everything we've got,* and He stretches and multiplies it, making it into more than we could ever imagine. Many times, though, we never get that far. We look at our limited resources and just give up. Like Andrew we wonder, *"What are these for so many?"* And we hang our heads in defeat when God is just waiting to supply our needs and give us victory like we would never believe.

LEARNING WHEN TO SIT DOWN

Jesus took a different approach than Philip and Andrew. His response to Andrew is found in John 6:10: "Have the people sit down." Then He gives thanks and breaks the bread. By the time the crowd was through eating, each person had their fill, and there were still twelve baskets left over. I find it funny that before

Jesus performed His miracle He asked the people to sit down. When I read this passage I always wonder if the boy with the lunch is one of those Jesus asked to sit down.

When you are sitting down you are in somewhat of a helpless position. You are in a position of relaxation, not action. There's not much you can do when you are sitting down. When Jesus told the hungry multitudes to sit down, everyone else had already done their part. The disciples had already come to Jesus with a need, and a boy with a lunch had been found (although some commentators say he may have been there to *sell* the bread and the fish).[2] All that was left to do was feed the crowd, and that was *Jesus'* job.

He no longer needed anyone else's help—He didn't even *need* their help in the beginning. He simply chose to involve them in the unfolding of a miracle. The same is true of us. Elisabeth Elliot once said:

> *Here lies the tremendous mystery—that God should be all-powerful, yet refuse to coerce. He summons us to cooperation. We are honored in being given the opportunity to participate in His good deeds. Remember how He asked for help in performing His miracles: Fill the water pots, stretch out your hand, distribute the loaves.*[3]

There comes a time when our work is done and everything left to do is up to God alone. How many times has God come to each of us, with our limited resources, and asked us to do one simple thing and then sit down? That's how God works. We come to Him saying, "Oh, Lord, I don't have much to give. But I do have something." He asks us for our "something," and He then takes it and multiplies it, making it fit for a multitude—as He did with the loaves and fish, Anna's vision of a girls' purity event, and Britany's Bible study.

The greatness never lies in the servant herself.

The secret to being a servant of God who sees great things unfold before her very eyes is found in recognizing—and accepting—that the greatness never lies in the servant herself but in her God. We are only responsible for giving our five loaves and two fish—it's all we are called to give because it is all we are ever capable of giving. God is not going to ask us to do things we cannot do, although He may ask us to *help* Him do things we could never do on our own.

Most of the time the things God asks us for are simple— they are everyday things we would carry around in a lunch sack, so to speak. He asks us to do something relatively easy, like give Him our time and resources or open our home or our heart to someone in need. He asks for faithfulness—and sometimes boldness—to step up and offer ourselves to Him, allowing Him to use us as He pleases.

Sometimes it will make the difference in the lives of many, as it did with Anna, Britany, and the boy with the fish and loaves. Other times it may only make a difference in the life of one person. But who knows how many lives will be changed as a result of the life of the one you helped to change. Don't underestimate trivial things—I mean, come on, we're talking about a God who uses sack lunches here. You can't get more trivial than that.

In high school I invited my friend Eric to church camp, and he got saved. After graduation we lost touch, but several years later I heard through a mutual friend that Eric had become a missionary in South America. I'm sure many lives have been touched by Eric, and it all started with a simple invitation to a weekend winter camp with my youth group.

Missionary Warren Webster once said, "If I had my life to live over again, I would live to change the lives of people, because you have not changed anything until you've changed the lives of people."[4]

When serving Christ, don't get so caught up in wanting to be a part of a miracle that you forget to simply serve other people.

Stand Up, Sit Down, Um, Which One Do I Do Now?

The trickiest part of learning to serve God is found in knowing when to stand up and share your lunch and when to sit down and let God work. But if we can remember the lessons learned in the first two chapters of this book—and we know how to listen to God—then we will know the difference.

When He wants our help He comes to us like He did Philip and asks, "Where are we to buy bread, that these may eat?" I can almost see a smile pulling at the corners of Jesus' mouth as

He asked Philip this question. He knew what Philip's answer would be.

"I'll take it from here."

When it's time for us to simply watch God unfold a miracle, His words to us are usually pretty clear: "Daughter, sit down. Rest awhile. I'll take it from here." So often in our success-driven culture we are taught to believe that we have failed if we have not completed a certain task from start to finish. But God himself knows that miracles aren't our business, and neither are results. Attitudes of servitude and the giving of the resources God has blessed us with are all God requires from His servants—well, those things and surrendered obedience. Remember, we find our lives by giving them away.

A man by the name of Norman Cousins once said, "History is willing to overlook almost anything—errors, paradoxes, personal weaknesses or faults—if only a man will give enough of himself to others."[5]

So give all you've got, but most important, remember to give yourself to God and those around you. Unlike other people, God does not ask more from you than you are able to give. It's not His intention to wear you out, stress you out, or burn you out. His desire is simply to invite you into the realm of miracles by asking you for simple things like your lunch, and then asking you to sit down and watch as the miracle unfolds.

What's in your lunch sack today, and when was the last time you offered it to meet a gigantic need? Once you give it to God, don't forget to sit down and rest. He'll take it from there, and you'll be amazed at what He is able to do with so little.

FOR FURTHER THOUGHT:

1. Why do you think the feeding of the five thousand is recorded in all four gospels?

2. What is the "sack lunch" God has given you to offer back to Him for His glory?

3. Are you more like Philip, Andrew, or the little boy with the lunch in your response to Jesus?

4. In what areas of your life has the Lord recently asked you to "sit down"?

5. Why do you think God allows us to help Him with His miracles?

TAKING THE CHALLENGE:

Find a need this week in which you have something to offer. Give what little you have to God and watch as He multiplies it for His glory.

Or

Find an area in your life where you are always trying to do things your own way, then stop and sit down and let God work as He pleases.

Notes

1. Adam Clarke, *Adam Clarke's Commentary on the New Testament*. CD-ROM. Quick Verse Deluxe, Version 7. Parsons Church Group, 2000–2001.
2. Ibid.
3. Daily Christian Quote [*http://psalm121.ca/quotes/dcqarchive402 .html*] April 27, 2002.
4. As quoted in Charles Swindoll's *The Tale of the Tardy Ox Cart* (Nashville, TN: Word Publishing, 1998), 300.
5. Ibid., 513.

9

If These Walls Could Speak

When I graduated from college I moved back home with my parents to continue working on my writing career. Being young when my first book was released, I knew writing wouldn't make me rich, but I still wanted to pursue the awesome opportunity God had placed before me. If I wanted to do this, I knew I wouldn't have much money to make ends meet. Since I was still single, I moved into the den in my parents' new home.

My room only had three solid walls. The other wall was made out of shutters that opened into the living room. I could hear everything that went on in the house, and the whole house could hear everything that went on in my room. (And I thought having roommates in college created a lack of privacy!) I lived there for just short of two years—until I got married. It was during that time that I grew to understand how powerful walls really are.

Sometimes in life God asks us to rise to the task of building a much-needed wall, as He did with Nehemiah. Other times God asks us to take on the seemingly impossible task of taking the walls down, as He did with Joshua. And sometimes we take it upon ourselves to erect and tear down walls as we please, walling people (and sometimes even God) in and out of our lives.

Certain walls protect us—like the walls that keep prisoners in prison and strangers out of our homes. Or even like metaphorical walls that keep us from giving our hearts away to some smooth-talking Romeo a little too quickly.

Other walls tend to block our paths—like the fact that we have to achieve a certain GPA and SAT score before we can be accepted into the college of our choice, or needing a certain level of physical stamina in order to get a spot on a competitive sports team. Metaphorical walls can make it hard to get through to someone we love, or make it hard for us to allow other people to love us. But one thing is certain: Walls can become very powerful tools in the hands of God if we learn to use them as a way of serving the Lord.

BUILDING FROM SCRATCH

Sometimes, as we seek to be girls who serve the Lord, He asks us to build something from nothing. This has been something that has always frustrated me, even though I have seen God be faithful in this area over and over again. How on earth are we ever supposed to build something *out of nothing*?

In the book of Nehemiah we are told of a sad situation— the once splendid city of Jerusalem had been ransacked by her enemies and burned with fire. As a result, Jerusalem's defensive wall had been torn down and the people living there were

BEING A GIRL WHO SERVES

defenseless. They could never rebuild their city without first rebuilding their wall. This situation grieved Nehemiah so much that he asked God to grant him favor with the pagan king he served. As the king's cupbearer, Nehemiah had a special access to him that other Jewish captives did not enjoy. His desire was that he might return to the city, help rebuild the wall, and so restore order to his homeland.

The next time he went in to see the king, the king noticed Nehemiah's sad face and asked him the reason. When he briefly mentioned the situation that made him so sad, the king asked, "What would you request?" Nehemiah 2:4 tells us Nehemiah "prayed to the God of heaven" at this point, asking what it was he should ask of the king. And then he asked the king to allow him to go to Jerusalem and rebuild the wall. God answered Nehemiah's prayer to give him favor, and he was sent on his way.

This is important to note because many times, when we *serve* the Lord, we don't *seek* the Lord. We rush ahead into situations, trying to do what we think is best without asking God what He would have us do. This always results in a huge mess. Nehemiah sure got things right when he sought God before he set out to serve. He also made a good move by asking God for favor with the king. We should ask God to grant us favor when we go before people in authority, to ask for their permission to do something God has called us to do.

In his bestselling book *Finding Favor With the King*, Tommy Tenney says, "Favor is what happens when preparation meets opportunity. Success is what happens when preparation meets potential. . . . One day of favor can be worth more than a life-time of labor."[1]

Many times as we seek to serve God in our own lives, He will bring needs to our attention that grieve us, like He did with Nehemiah. We see children going hungry in foreign countries, and our hearts are stirred to become part of their monthly sponsorship team through organizations such as World Vision and Compassion International. We hear that there is no teacher for one of the classes at our church's annual summer Vacation Bible School program, so we step up to teach for a week or two. Our church is taking a trip to an orphanage in Mexico and we start noticing all of the clothes and shoes that we never wear bursting out of our closets, so we donate several items to be taken to children who literally have nothing.

Yes, those things have some cost to them. And they are excellent ways to give of ourselves to serve the Lord. But what about all of the times when the need we see has no immediate solution? What about the times when we are called to build something from scratch like Nehemiah?

Meeting a Need—and So Much More

In high school there was a time when there was nobody to disciple me or any of the other girls in my youth group. I prayed and prayed, asking God to do something about it. Finally He showed me to start a small girls' discipleship group in my own home. Eventually, many of the girls in that group went on to lead discipleship groups of their own. But when I first went to

BEING A GIRL WHO SERVES

my youth pastor with the idea, I had no clue how he was going to respond to the idea of me, a mere sophomore, leading a group of girls—several of which were older than me.

Even though I was young, God used me to build something that was far bigger than me—something that went on long after I ended my group and moved on. And many girls were touched and changed as a result.

Later, God asked me to start a similar group with junior high girls, some of who also went on to lead their own groups. And when I was in college He had me start yet another girls' Bible study. Each time, the people who were touched and changed as a result of being part of the group God asked me to start, went on and touched and changed others. As I started to build something from the ground up, God surrounded me with other faithful servants who joined me, making the task not only easier but more fruitful as well.

There was once a woman of incredible faith named Henrietta Mears. She was able to see past obstacles and built many "walls" from scratch. She taught college-age single people for decades at Hollywood Presbyterian Church. She was a formative influence on the life of a whole generation of Christian leaders, including Billy Graham.

She was frustrated at not being able to give her students top-notch materials to help them grow on their own, outside of their class. So she began a small publishing business out of her own garage. It grew into Gospel Light Publishers—one of the most effective Christian publishers of its day. Ms. Mears is also responsible for founding Forest Home Christian Camp in Southern California and writing a single volume introduction to the Bible that has sold hundreds of thousands of copies. This book was even one of Michael's textbooks in Bible college. Those three important accomplishments were all walls that Ms. Mears was asked to build from scratch—and she did.[2] With God's strength and God's power, she did. We could have a similar impact if only we would step forward in faith and let God use us.

WHISTLING WHILE YOU WORK

Whenever we set out to serve the Lord, whether we are seeking to create something new or build on something that already exists, we are bound to receive opposition and some heckling. People are just mean; even other Christians can be mean at times. And many people tend to look down on those who are doing what they would never dare to do—especially if those doing the work are younger than them. First Timothy 4:12 (NKJV) says, "Let no one despise your youth" for a reason.

In Nehemiah 4, Nehemiah and his friends began to be taunted by people who told them their wall could easily be destroyed again, or that they would never finish the task. Certain groups even conspired to attack Nehemiah and his friends in an attempt to destroy their work. In Nehemiah 4:9 he says, "But we prayed to our God, and because of them we set up a guard against them day and night."

This is an important tool in fighting the devil. If we can

learn to pray to the Lord, asking Him for His help, and if we can learn to sing praises to our great and mighty God, the voices of those heckling (and even threatening) us will not be able to be heard over our loud and lively worship!

So when you set out to be a girl who serves, and you start to hear some heckling, simply offer a prayer up to the Lord and sing praises to Him as loudly as you possibly can. Trust me, your foes will eventually become so frustrated that they will quit and leave you alone. But they don't always give up easily.

Well-known worship leader Matt Redman once said, "The heart of God loves a persevering worshipper who, though overwhelmed by many troubles, is overwhelmed even more by the beauty of God."[3]

> *"God loves a persevering worshipper."*

We need to be unquenchable worshipers who whistle while we work. We need to shout out praises to God for His greatness, no matter what. Don't let your enemy intimidate you from worshiping Him all day long. In her *Living Beyond Yourself* Bible study, Beth Moore said, "I like to give God a standing ovation because when we give Him a standing ovation He is more likely to give an encore." She talked about how she literally applauds God when He does something great in her life. It's a habit I am in the process of picking up. Now I not only whistle and sing while I work, I've also been known to break out in spontaneous clapping.

When the Enemy Strikes

When Nehemiah was nearly finished with building the wall, a group of jealous people plotted to harm him. *Four* times they attempted to get him to come down from the wall and stop what he was doing. Persistently they badgered him, and when his strength was weak, Nehemiah went to the Lord and prayed, "O God, strengthen my hands" (6:9). Sometimes those out to destroy us are the most unlikely people—sometimes they are even our brothers and sisters in Christ.

If you are doing something that will greatly impact the kingdom of God, of course the devil is going to try to stop it. And *he will use anyone he can to help him.* It's been said that opposition can be viewed as a confirmation that you are heading in the right direction. The devil never wants to stop his own work, but he always wants to stop God's.

When I was in college I led a mission trip, and as the team leader it was my responsibility to make sure our support letters were written and sent before our six-week Christmas break. Having a twenty-five-person team, this was not an easy task. But I managed to get it done—with four days to spare. So I went by the office and dropped off my letters, then went back to my dorm to pack my things to go home for Christmas break.

Meanwhile, the person in charge of postage and getting the letters mailed purposely let them sit around until it was far too late to get them in the mail. This person was not part of my team, and apparently he thought things were coming along just a little too easily for me. Since we were the only team to meet the deadline, he thought we should have to wait and suffer the six-week penalty everyone else did. He also had a heart for another geographic region and didn't think my trip was as important. It bothered him that my team was roughly ten times the size of his. He didn't realize it wasn't about numbers but about who God had called to minister.

When I found out about the letters I was livid. I went to this person and confronted him. He was rude to me and made some snide remark about how sometimes things just don't work out how we planned. I called the post office and tried to take care of things myself, but this person refused to give the letters back to me.

When someone else confronted him on it, he began to back-pedal. He realized that twenty-five people would now have six weeks less to raise their support for a trip that was all about God's glory. Several months later, our team was the only team to raise all of our support—and several thousand dollars extra. This person who had tried to oppose us had to stand back and know that God refused to let someone else foil *His* plans.

In Nehemiah's case, the wall was rebuilt. In my case, the support money was raised. In your case God will come through for you and give you the victory if you stand back and let Him. Don't lose your temper—I probably got a little more heated than I should have. Seek God like Nehemiah did, let God be your defense, and in the end your wall will stand tall for all—including those who attempted to ruin your plans—to see.

In the book of Nehemiah, Jerusalem was restored. God

conquered those who were in opposition to His plans. He silenced them and put them in their place. Nehemiah is an excellent example of how to handle the frustration of trying to build something from the ground up. He let God be his strength and defender. I would strongly encourage you to read Nehemiah's entire story sometime.

> ## He let God be his strength and defender.

For me, watching God supply the funding for my team, in spite of losing six vital weeks for raising support (we only had twelve or thirteen weeks total—counting those six weeks), taught me a lot about trusting God. It makes me wonder if He allows frustrations like that simply for that purpose. Nothing is as exciting as setting out and attempting to do something people say cannot be done, then watching God come through for you in spite of setbacks and adverse circumstances. One of the greatest rewards of being a girl who serves is watching God do for you what only God can.

JUST LIKE JERICHO

Sometimes in life there are walls God desires to tear down rather than build up. In Joshua's day, God desired to level the walls surrounding the sinful city of Jericho. In our lives sometimes God wants us to help get rid of walls surrounding hard-hearted people who are not open to God's love. Or He wants us to help tear down walls that are dictating where the Gospel can and cannot go.

In my short life I have met many girls who have watched God break down huge walls before their very eyes. During college my friend Sam went on a trip with one other girl. Their goal was to smuggle Bibles into China. Everyone in the customs line was getting his or her bags searched. Sam watched this in horror, knowing that if the Chinese government found the Bibles in her suitcase she would be in big trouble—and the Bibles would be confiscated.

"Lord, make me invisible," she prayed silently as her knees shook with fear. The security officer searched the bags of the person in front of her and then immediately went to the person behind her, skipping over Sam completely. Because of that Sam was able to get over a wall blocking the Gospel. She had the joy of handing the Bibles out to persecuted Christians who desperately needed them.

Another girl I know who is an American of Hispanic descent became a missionary in a South American country. A year or so into her adventure, she began to sense God's calling to the Middle East. She went to an area where Americans were generally disliked and Christians were definitely not allowed. Because she spoke fluent Spanish, and had dark hair, dark eyes, and beautiful olive skin, they took her for a South American and she was welcomed into the country as a schoolteacher. (Of course, the government knew she was an American because of her passport. But all of the locals and insurgents were fooled.)

God broke down incredible barriers for her by routing her through another country.

Don't be intimidated to stand up and do things God has called you to do, even if they seem impossible and there is a huge wall blocking your way.

Walking in Circles

My dog used to amuse herself at times by running in circles, chasing her own tail. After a while she'd get dizzy and wobble around a bit before lying down. As a person, nothing is more annoying—or nauseating—than going around in circles. Sometimes, though, God directs His children to do just that. Look at what He says to Joshua in Joshua 6:1–3:

> Now Jericho was tightly shut because of the sons of Israel; no one came out and no one came in. And the Lord said to Joshua, "See, I have given Jericho into your hand, with its king and the valiant warriors. And you shall march around the city, all the men of war circling the city once. You shall do so for six days."

Why on earth would God ever ask us to walk in circles? Have you ever felt like no matter how far you go and how much you do, you always seem to find yourself back in the very same spot? I know I have.

When I moved away to college, the one thing I always said I would never, ever do was move back home after I graduated. I was adamant. There was just no way. There was nothing left for me in the small town I came from. I was sure of that much. But three and a half years later, when my college graduation came and went and I found myself looking at a lucrative job opportunity near where I went to school and an internship on the East Coast, something deep inside me told me God wanted me to go back home. I argued with Him at first, and finally, weary from the fight, I went back home to live with my parents (as you already know from the beginning of this chapter). Once there, I spent a year building the *Being a Girl* Bible study program for junior and senior high girls, and I met my husband.

Had God not taken me in a complete circle—against my own will—I would be at a huge loss and I would have missed out on a big part of God's plan for my life. When God says to move in circles, He's got a purpose behind it. Sometimes it's to teach us patience, other times it's so we can pick up something we missed the first time around. Trust me, He doesn't do it so He can sit in heaven and laugh at us, the way I laughed at my silly dog.

But the whole walking in circles thing is not even the weirdest part of God's command to Joshua. Look at what happened next in verses 4–6 of chapter 6:

> Also seven priests shall carry seven trumpets of rams' horns before the ark; then on the seventh day you shall march around the city seven times, and the priests shall blow the trumpets. And it shall be that when they make a long

blast with the ram's horn, and when you hear the sound of the trumpet, all the people shall shout with a loud shout; and the wall of the city will fall down flat, and the people will go up every man straight ahead.

Huh? Is it just me or does that sound strange to anyone else? The people were supposed to walk around the city for six days, and on the seventh day they were to blow rams' horns and shout. Weird. It just makes no sense whatsoever. But sometimes that is how God works.

Sometimes as servants of God, He asks us to do seemingly odd things—things that just don't make any logical sense. Maybe God is asking you to quit playing a sport you love, and when you obey, an incredible opportunity will come your way that you could never have imagined. Perhaps He is asking you to spend your next holiday break visiting with family members who are difficult and odd. You never know what kind of impact you may have on them.

Whatever it is God is asking you to do, if it sounds strange, don't worry. Just do it. We can never see what God is truly doing until He has actually done it. There is always more to His plans than meets the eye.

In each of our lives there will be a time of building walls and tearing walls down. As we seek to serve the Lord, there will be times when we are to start new things and times when we are to finish off old things. Both require a great amount of faith. Neither can be done on your own. One isn't harder than the other—both are equal tasks. What you learn doing one may be valuable to you when the time comes for you to do the other.

In the end, it doesn't matter whether you are being asked to build a wall or knock one down, as long as you are prayerfully seeking God through the process and letting Him be your defense. But whatever you do, don't grumble when He asks you to walk in circles or do something that sounds a little weird. At times like that just smile to yourself and think, *I know something no one else does*: A miracle is most certainly on its way.

FOR FURTHER THOUGHT:

1. What walls do you see in your life right now?

2. Are you being called to build walls or knock them down? How so?

3. Who are those who are ridiculing your efforts? How do you plan to keep going in light of their comments?

4. What are some ways in which you feel you have been walking in circles lately?

5. Has God ever asked you to do anything weird? If so, what? How did it turn out?

TAKING THE CHALLENGE:

Find an area in your life where God is asking you to start something new and begin taking steps to accomplish the task. Seek God's will and then ask Him to grant you favor. Get permission from those you need permission from and start assembling a team.

If there's a wall in your life you need to tear down, then apply the same principles and get to it. Serve God in a way that no one around you seems to be serving at the moment. Look for an unmet need—and if God shows you, begin to serve Him by building that wall or tearing it down. Let all that you do be done as unto the Lord!

Notes

1. Tommy Tenney, *Finding Favor With the King* (Minneapolis, MN: Bethany House Publishers, 2003), 157, 36.
2. As told in John Ortberg's *If You Want to Walk on Water, You've Got to Get Out of the Boat* (Grand Rapids, MI: Zondervan, 2001), 88.
3. Matt Redman, *The Unquenchable Worshipper* (Ventura, CA: Regal Books, 2001), 25.

10

True Servants Wear Red

Most people who know me well may be surprised by the title of this chapter. *Pink* is my favorite color in the entire world, so they would assume that I would say true servants wear pink. But I would rather wear red than pink any day. Let me explain myself.

The greatest servants of all are those who have learned how to make prayer a lifestyle, not a ritual. By making it a lifestyle they spend countless hours on their knees in prayer, seeking God's intervention in the lives of those they know (or sometimes don't know). This is known as intercessory prayer—praying on behalf of someone else. It is one of the easiest ways to serve God and others, yet often it goes undone.

Although all of us have prayed for someone else at one time or another, it would be safe to say that few of us have *persisted* in those prayers. Those who do persevere exemplify a rare characteristic of true servants. They wear red because they have "bloody knees." Wearing red is simply a metaphor for a life lived in prayer. If you are constantly on your knees they are bound to become raw and worn.

For those of us living in the United States, the concept of

having bloody knees is not literal (if it were, it would not be very appealing) because we have the comfort of carpeted floors and we don't always have to kneel to pray. But I like what the phrase suggests. You wouldn't get bloody knees from kneeling gently once or twice. The only way to have a prayer life that would merit bloody knees is by constantly throwing yourself to your knees in prayer, seeking God fervently through all of life's ups and downs.

LEARNING TO LOOK FOR SACRED SANCTUARIES

Most servants will spend hours upon hours of their lives in prayer. You may not have several extra hours in every day, but if you are going to become an intercessor, you must learn to "steal" the minutes. I begin each morning with prayer and reading my Bible and a devotional book. But I also pray throughout my day. For me, both my car and my shower have proven to be intimate sanctuaries for God and me to meet in prayer, since I venture to both of those places on a regular basis. That's why being a prayer warrior is one of the easiest ministries to engage in—you can do it anytime, anywhere, and with anyone.

Think for a moment about the places you pass through every day that could become sacred sanctuaries if you would simply let them. I've already mentioned the car and the shower, but what about spending time in prayer during a workout routine or as you are doing your chores? Sacred sanctuaries exist everywhere. We just have to learn to look for them. I once knew a guy who spent time praying for certain missionaries every night when he brushed his teeth. He always remembered to pray as long as he remembered to brush his teeth.

S. D. Gordon once said, "You can do more than pray, after you have prayed. But you cannot do more than pray *until* you have prayed."[1] So many times, when we set out to be servants, we think we have to do this and do that. We can easily get bogged down with starting a certain ministry or witnessing to a certain number of people. Sometimes we even stress ourselves out trying to be perfect Christians. But none of that matters if we are not spending time with the Lord.

We cannot effectively serve others if we have not learned to imitate Christ, and the Bible tells us that Christ himself intercedes on our behalf. One of the prime examples of Christ praying for one of His own is found in Luke 22:31–32 when Jesus says to Peter, "Simon, Simon, behold, Satan has demanded permission to sift you like wheat; but I have prayed for you, that your faith may not fail."

Hebrews 7:25 tells us that Christ makes intercession for those who draw near to Him. Think about how many times, like Peter, the enemy has come against us with everything he has and we desperately need someone to be praying that our faith will not fail. There are countless moments in all of our lives that drive us to prayer. But imagine the results we would see if two or three gather together in the fight to pray for the salvation, healing, or deliverance of someone they love.

PRAYER CHANGES THINGS

There was a woman in our church who received a heart transplant not that long ago. She had been sick for a very long time, and things grew very bleak for her. It did not look like she was going to pull through. But many in our congregation joined together in the fight to intercede on her behalf. Day and night we asked God to provide her with a new heart or to heal the one she had. She was placed on the transplant list, on which many people spend months or years before getting a new heart.

However, within three short days she had a heart! With her frail body frame she was able to accept a heart that was much too small for all of those ahead of her on the list. One of the surgeons told her how fortunate she was to get a heart so quickly, because he had a family member who had been on the list for a very long time. I honestly believe that God gave this woman a heart because His people joined together and prayed. Several months later I found out this woman had prayed for God to give her the heart of a Christian so she could rest knowing that her donor was in heaven. When the allotted time passed for grieving and she was allowed to contact the donor's family, she found that God had answered her prayers by giving her a heart belonging to another Christian. God not only answers prayers; sometimes He answers very specific prayers.

Although we can never force God through prayer to do whatever we want Him to, we can intercede knowing that as long as we are praying according to His will, He will answer us.

Recently I attended a marriage conference where the speaker

encouraged wives to set time aside and pray specifically for their husbands every day for thirty days. Today I set ten minutes aside to pray specifically for Michael's job. As soon as my ten minutes was done, my cell phone rang and it was Michael telling me he had experienced two great victories at work within the past ten minutes. I was so stunned I could barely speak.

Sure, I expected God to answer—but that was quicker than a UPS overnight delivery! It definitely motivated me to keep wearing red day after day as I pray for my husband. But we should be equally motivated to keep praying even when we do not see instant results. I know many people who prayed for unsaved family members for years before seeing results. But through God's mighty power and their bloody knees, those loved ones eventually came to Christ.

There is a true disheartening account of what one woman let her seemingly unanswered prayers do to her just after World War II:

> Roger Simms, hitchhiking his way home, would never forget the date—May 7. His heavy suitcase made Roger tired. He was anxious to take off his army uniform once and for all. Flashing the hitchhiking sign to the oncoming car, he lost hope when he saw it was a black sleek new Cadillac. To his surprise the car stopped. The passenger door opened. He ran toward the car, tossed his suitcase in the back, and thanked the handsome, well-dressed man as he slid into the front seat.
>
> "Going home for keeps?"

"Sure am," Roger responded.

"Well, you're in luck if you are going to Chicago."

"Not quite that far. Do you live in Chicago?"

"I have a business there. My name is Hanover."

After talking about many things, Roger, a Christian, felt a compulsion to witness to this fiftyish, apparently successful businessman about Christ. But he kept putting it off, till he realized he was just thirty minutes from his home. It was now or never. So Roger cleared his throat. "Mr. Hanover, I would like to talk to you about something very important." He then proceeded to explain the way of salvation, ultimately asking Mr. Hanover if he would like to receive Christ as his Savior. To Roger's astonishment the Cadillac pulled over to the side of the road. Roger thought he was going to be ejected from the car. But the businessman bowed his head and received Christ, then thanked Roger. "This is the greatest thing that has ever happened to me."

Five years went by, Roger married, had a two-year-old boy, and a business of his own. Packing his suitcase for a business trip to Chicago, he found the small, white, business card Hanover had given him five years before.

In Chicago he looked up Hanover Enterprises. A receptionist told him it was impossible to see Mr. Hanover, but he could see Mrs. Hanover. A little confused as to what was going on, he was ushered into a lovely office and found himself facing a keen-eyed woman in her fifties. She extended her hand, "You knew my husband?"

Roger told her how her husband had given him a ride when hitchhiking home after the war.

BEING A GIRL WHO SERVES

"Can you tell me when that was?"

"It was May 7, five years ago, the day I was discharged from the army."

"Anything special about that day?"

Roger hesitated . . . should he mention his witness? Since he had come so far, he might as well take the plunge. "Mrs. Hanover, I explained the gospel. He pulled over to the side of the road and wept against the steering wheel. He gave his life to Christ that day."

Explosive sobs shook her body. Getting a grip on herself, she sobbed, "I had prayed for my husband's salvation for years. I believed God would save him."

"And," said Roger, "where is your husband, Mrs. Hanover?"

"He's dead," she wept, struggling with the words. "He was in a car crash after he let you out of the car. He never got home. You see—I thought God had not kept His promise." Sobbing uncontrollably, she added, "I stopped living for God five years ago because I thought He had not kept His word."[2]

We cannot stop praying because we do not see results, and we most certainly cannot stop believing in God and His Word when we do not see any results. Because whether or not we can see it, God is always at work someway and somehow, bringing His perfect will to pass.

I want to challenge you to pick one person in your life and start praying something specific over their lives for ten minutes every day. Pick a certain time—like when you brush your teeth or wash your hair—and pray for that person at that time every single day. Choose to wear red on their behalf, and I am sure you will be amazed by the results.

For Better, for Worse

Most of us complain about prayer—that there is not enough time in the day to pray, it is just too hard to pray while we are doing other things, too difficult to pray when we are trying to wake up in the morning or go to bed at night because we always wind up falling asleep before we say "amen," and so on. But those are all excuses, not reasons, why we don't pray as we should.

All over the world there are Christians who gather to pray in underground churches in countries where they could be killed for their faith. These people have legitimate *reasons* why they can't pray—or at least not pray out loud—and yet they do it anyway. This silences all of our complaints, doesn't it?

In the Bible there are many examples of prayer warriors. The psalms are full of David's prayers to God through both the good times and the bad. In Psalm 109:30 he says:

With my mouth I will give thanks abundantly to the LORD; and in the midst of many I will praise Him.

Psalm 62:1–2 says:

My soul waits in silence for God only; from Him is my salvation. He only is my rock and my salvation, my stronghold; I shall not be greatly shaken.

These are the prayers of a man who knew where to draw his strength from and how to pray in an unrestrained manner. They are the prayers of a man who knew help always comes from one place and one place alone: God. Throughout the psalms we can read the prayers of David's heart when he was a shepherd boy tending his flock, a fugitive running from a mad king, a king seeking wisdom, and a broken sinner pleading for forgiveness for committing adultery and murder.

David knew how to pray, and I am not talking about the poetry of his words. I am talking about the *condition of his heart.* He knew that no matter what state he was in or what was going on in his life, God would lead him forward if he simply asked. He sought God for his own sake, but we also find him pleading before the Lord on behalf of a son who would eventually die, and seeking blessing for the people of Israel.

David was a servant king. Although imperfect, he was an excellent king. The Bible even tells us he was a man after God's own heart. David wore red, and he wore it often. He knew how to serve in a great capacity because he knew how to kneel. When was the last time you took some time to kneel?

Maybe you have an easy time praying for yourself when things are going pretty crummy. You call upon God when your friends abandon you, you are not getting along with your siblings, and your parents are too busy to listen to your petitions. But you have a hard time beseeching Him on behalf of others. You just have too much going on in your own life to worry about other people.

The night Jesus told Peter He was praying for him because Satan desired to sift him like wheat, they were standing in the Garden of Gethsemane. It was just days before Jesus would be crucified. I'm sure He had better things to do than pray for Peter. Yet praying for Peter was at the forefront of His mind. As His disciples, praying for others should always be at the forefront of our minds too.

TALKING GOD'S EAR OFF

God loves it when we pray. After all, He created prayer as our means of being able to communicate with Him. Oswald Chambers once said, "We look upon prayer as a means of getting things for ourselves; the Bible's idea of prayer is that we may get to know God Himself."[3]

> *We serve others best when we pray for them.*

As girls who seek to serve others, that should be our highest aim. May it be said of us at the end of our lives that we knew God and that we spent many hours throughout our lives in deep conversation with Him. Serving others through prayer will be the natural result of a person who seeks God with all her heart. We serve others best when we pray for them before we do anything else.

One of the greatest examples of someone who lived a life

of intercessory prayer is a woman by the name of Fern Nichols. She is the founder of a ministry called Moms In Touch International. The background of her ministry is described this way on her Web site:

In the fall of 1984 Fern Nichols' two oldest children of four were entering junior high school. Her heart was heavy and burdened with concern as she knew they would be facing their greatest test in resisting immoral values, vulgar language, peer pressure, and philosophies that would undermine their faith. She cried out to the Lord, asking Him to protect them, enable them to see clearly the difference between right and wrong, and make good decisions.

The burden to intercede for her boys was overwhelming. She asked God to give her another mom who felt the same burden, and who would be willing to pray with her concerning their children and their school. God heard the cry of her heart and led her to another mom who shared her burden. Others were invited to come and they began meeting the following week for prayer.

This was the beginning of Moms In Touch International—moms in touch with God, their children, their schools, and one another through prayer. As moms began sharing what God had been doing in their lives and in the lives of their children through prayer, other groups began to spring up all over British Columbia where they were living at the time.

The summer of 1985 brought a change to Fern's family as they moved from Abbotsford, British Columbia to Poway,

California. She soon discovered that God had given her still greater opportunities for carrying on the work that began in Canada. Once again she prayed that God would raise up moms who were willing to "stand in the gap" for their children. That fall, Fern began the first MITI group for Poway High School, and soon many other groups began to form for schools in that district. This grassroots effort spread quickly as moms prayed for groups to start around the state and across the nation.

The fall of 1987 brought the first published Moms In Touch booklet, and in January of 1988 the first Moms In Touch retreat was held with 35 women. They prayed for national exposure and God answered their prayers that spring when Fern got a call from a producer at Focus on the Family and by May she and twelve other moms were on the air talking to Dr. Dobson! That first radio program brought over 20,000 responses.

Today, there are Moms In Touch groups in every state of the United States, and representatives in over 110 foreign countries around the world.[4]

The reason Fern's ministry stands out to me in such a powerful way is because it is a ministry my mom served in for years. When I was in kindergarten my mom started a Moms In Touch group for my school. The next year we moved, so she started another group at my new school. At the end of the school year we moved again, so my mom started yet another group. That year we stopped moving—but God didn't. For the next several years of my life—all the way until middle school—God had the school board restructure the boundary lines, causing me to go to a new school every year so that my mom could start a new prayer group.

For middle school I was able to stay put, and the summer before I began high school, my mom started a group for the local school I was scheduled to attend. But, surprise, we moved again and my mom started a group for the high school I eventually did attend. There were a total of seven or eight prayer groups that sprang from my own mother's willingness to follow Fern Nichols' lead. And the results were incredible.

We had unsaved teachers coming to my mom for prayer. The moms in her prayer group were asked to preview all of the new school books before they were placed in the school library. At every school I attended, the administrators knew my mom well. They liked her and they appreciated her. Because of that, many of them liked me. I was the girl with the mom who prayed. And that is a legacy I have never forgotten. Although I am not yet a mom myself, I have been impacted by the many ways my mom has prayed for me over the years, and as a result I have tried my hardest to pray fervently for others as well.

Lives change when we pray. Whether it is obvious to us in the beginning or not, God shakes both heaven and earth when His children join together and seek His face. In 2 Chronicles 7:14 He says, "If . . . My people who are called

Lives change when we pray.

by My name humble themselves and pray, and seek My face, and turn from their wicked ways, then I will hear from heaven, will forgive their sin, and will heal their land."

That is a magnificent promise to hold on to. We need to be humbling ourselves and praying on behalf of those around us. We need to be *intercessory servants* who aren't afraid to wear red as we pray for our friends, our families, our schools, our nation, and the nations surrounding us. The call is simple, really: just pray. Remember, we can do more than pray *after* we have prayed, but we cannot do more than pray *until* we have prayed.

So what are you waiting for? Get bloody knees.

FOR FURTHER THOUGHT:

1. What could the concept of wearing red realistically look like in your life?

2. How often do you pray? Are your prayers always petitions for yourself, or do you pray for others as well?

3. Dividing your prayer life into percentages, how often do you pray for yourself and how often do you pray for others?

4. Do you have a set time to pray each day? Why or why not?

5. Is it harder or easier for you to pray for people other than yourself? Why do you think that is?

Being a Girl Who Serves

TAKING THE CHALLENGE:

Find a sacred sanctuary in your life and try to go there once a day. Pray about the same thing or for the same person consistently every day for six months and wait in anticipation to see how God will work. Remember to pray according to His will—and please drop me an e-mail when you begin to see answers to your prayers. I love to keep a record of the faithfulness of God!

Notes

1. S. D. Gordon, *Quiet Talks on Prayer* (New York: Grosset & Dunlap/Revell, 1941), 16.
2. Ron Mehl, *Surprise Endings* (Sisters, OR: Multnomah Publishers, Inc., 1988), 9.
3. Oswald Chambers, *My Utmost for His Highest* (Westwood, NJ: Barbour & Co, 1935), August 28.
4. "A Brief History of Moms In Touch International," *www.momsintouch.org*, October 13, 2005.

11

All the Way to the Cross

I was raised in a Christian home. For as long as I can remember I have attended Sunday school classes. When I was two years old my mom tells me I came home from church reciting the story of Moses. Sometimes for people like me it is harder to grasp concepts like grace, redemption, and the true cost of the cross, because it is something we have heard since the day we were born.

The only thing shocking to us about the Gospel is how people think they can live without it. Yet we take it for granted every day of our lives. Sometimes it takes someone else's powerful conversion story to make us realize the magnitude of what Christ did for us and what it is that He *asks of us* in return. Recently I came across such a story.

Raised as a Hindu, Sadhu Sundar Singh came to a saving knowledge of Jesus Christ. Turning to Christ meant turning away from all he had ever known. And, like all radical converts, he had an excellent grasp on the sacrifices we as Christians are sometimes called to make. Believing in Christ cost him something, but he never once thought it wasn't worth it. Here's what he says:

It is easy to die for Christ. It is hard to live for Him. Dying takes only an hour or two, but to live for Christ means to die daily. Only during the few years of this life are we given the privilege of serving each other and Christ.... We shall have heaven forever, but only a short time of service here, and therefore we must not waste the opportunity.[1]

> *Serve the Lord with everything you've got today.*

Oh, to live like that! If I could sum up the concept of *Being a Girl Who Serves* in one sentence it would be this: Don't waste the time that you have—serve the Lord with everything you've got today. With each passing minute we are running out of time to serve the Lord. I'm not saying this to send us all into a frantic panic. I'm saying it because it is a reality.

THE TIME IS TICKING AWAY

When my husband and I were engaged, we each had a little clock sitting on our desks that would count down the days, hours, and minutes until our wedding day. We constantly joked with one another, saying things like, "Only one hundred and seventy-nine more days until we get to spend the rest of our lives together."

Too bad we don't have a clock like that to count down the days until we enter eternity. If we did, it might help us to use our time just a little more wisely. So often we do not live with purpose. We wander around through our high school and college years somewhat directionless. Life becomes too much about the mundane and ordinary: school, soccer practice, and work. It's not enough about what's truly important: leading those around us to the saving knowledge of Christ and the enjoyment of a relationship with Him.

We as Christians have no excuse to ever be without direction. We are to live lives pointed toward the cross every single day. We are to serve the Lord no matter the cost. Yet even a small fee we might have to pay for our faith—like being forsaken by friends or being called a "goody-goody" at school—often is enough to send us running in the opposite direction. We think, *There are far better ways we can find to use our time than being ripped apart and forsaken by those around us.*

But if our aim in life is to be like Jesus, and He willingly went to the cross for us, shouldn't we be willing to do the same? As girls we probably have three things in life that we are at least remotely afraid of: losing friends that we hold dear, being mocked and ridiculed for our beliefs, and dying young. None of these possibilities sounds appealing to any of us, I'm sure. And not all three of these things may be asked of us. But *they were all asked of Jesus,* and it would do us good to see how He responded to what God called Him to do in serving us.

Left All Alone

Throughout the last three years of Jesus' life there were many people—thousands, even—who flocked to Him. When people heard He was in town, they ran to meet Him at the city gates. Most wanted something from Him, while a few simply wanted to watch the excitement that accompanied His ministry. When Jesus was in town miracles were sure to follow.

But even with seeming popularity—or at least curiosity—among the masses, Jesus was very selective about whom He invited into His inner circle of twelve. Oddly enough, He entrusted His money to Judas. He invited James, Peter, and John into the inner recesses of the Garden of Gethsemane, asking them to stay up with Him and pray through the long night.

As we all know, Judas was the disciple who eventually betrayed Jesus. And Peter was the one who denied Him—not once, but three times. The inner circle of three, asked by Jesus to pray with Him, kept falling asleep that night. Matthew 26:56 tells us that when the Roman soldiers came to seize Jesus in the garden, all of His disciples "left Him and fled."

It was not just the miracle-seeking mobs that turned on Jesus when it came time for Him to face the cross. It was those in the carefully selected twelve—even the inner three—who deserted Jesus when it mattered most. Yet He boldly went forward to the cross, even when He had to go all alone. Can we say the same thing about ourselves?

When I was in high school I was hanging out with some non-Christian friends who were known to be among the most popular kids in school. I had a lot of classes with them over the years, and by my senior year we had done enough projects together that they began to invite me to hang out with them outside of school.

Prior to that, I had not been known as a nerd by any means, but I hadn't really been noticed by anyone other than my Christian friends either. I went to a large public high school where it was easy to slip in and out of the gates without drawing much attention to yourself. In my senior year all that changed for me.

There were many moments when I was uncomfortable hanging out with some of the "popular" kids. I didn't like the way a lot of the guys looked at or spoke to the girls, and their lives seemed to be an endless quest for a party. My convictions were different from theirs. I wanted to be popular, but not at the expense of everything I believed in and stood for.

So I didn't let my free ticket to popularity take me to all of the places it promised I could go. But by refusing to become part of the "in crowd," I could not go back to the obscurity I had known before. If I wasn't in, I was "out." And there were many who let me know it.

Another Christian girl in that crowd took the free ticket, cashing in on her childhood faith. The one and only time I was invited to her house I was amazed to find Bible verses and Christian posters covering the walls in her room—this girl used profanity, made out with a different guy every week, and was one of the biggest party girls on campus.

I sat staring at her walls in shock, pleading silently with God to prevent me from becoming such a hypocrite. When I went home that night I wanted very little to do with the world and the costly popularity it offered me. And I don't regret my decision, not even a little. Sure, I spent a lot of Friday nights alone in the weeks following my departure from the "in crowd," but I would take a night alone anytime over a night of regrets.

I reminded myself that I was headed toward the cross with determination and purpose because *I knew it's what Jesus had done for me.* We either walk boldly toward the cross, or we run away from it. We don't have the option of spinning around in circles, living for the Lord one day and partying with the world the next. We have to make up our mind as to which life we will choose to live.

Mocked and Ridiculed

On His way to the cross Jesus was mocked and ridiculed like we wouldn't believe. The Bible tells us He was yelled at and taunted, spit on, and beaten beyond recognition. Soldiers even gambled for His undergarments. How humiliating.

In junior high I knew some mean and obnoxious kids. Knowing I was a Christian, they razzed me about everything. One boy even dug through my backpack when I wasn't looking one day, pulled out a feminine hygiene product, and taped it to the wall during passing period with a sign that read, *This is Shannon Kubiak's.*

I was so mortified I never wanted to return to school again. There was a time when I gave in to the pressure and began to talk and dress like these other kids, just to get them off my back. For a while I cashed in on my faith and bought myself some peace at school. But it wasn't long before my small compromises weren't enough. My peers began to ask for more from me, and when I wasn't willing to do what they wanted, the ridicule returned. Only this time it was more intense.

Nothing is worse than being at a place like school—which you cannot easily run away from—and having to endure all kinds of harassment due to your faith. I meet a lot of girls who have painful stories. One junior higher I spoke with told me the worst part of her life was "the mean snots at school." Most of us would do anything to get the cruel banter and embarrassing moments to stop. But is cashing in on our faith really worth it? As Jesus hung on the cross dying for us He faced much worse. Mark 15:29–32 says:

> And those passing by were hurling abuse at Him, wagging their heads, and saying, "Ha! You who are going to destroy the temple and rebuild it in three days, save Yourself, and come down from the cross!" In the same way the chief priests also, along with the scribes, were mocking Him among themselves saying, "He saved others; He cannot save Himself. Let this Christ, the King of Israel, now come down from the cross, so that we may see and believe!" And those who were crucified with Him were casting the same insult at Him.

Our loving Savior silently endured both the verbal abuse and the physical pain that ripped through His body and slowly claimed His life. He made no defense. He let God have the last word and stayed on the cross. From Matthew 26:53 we know that He could have requested help from angels and been delivered from His torture. He could have copped out, but He chose to pay the full price for our redemption. Our crosses will never be that intense. Nothing could ever cost us as much as the cross cost Jesus because He died not for His own sins, but for ours.

He let God have the last word.

How many of us back down at lesser levels of mocking and ridicule? How many times will we cast aside our faith and turn away from the cross simply to avoid a pinprick of pain? Why is it that we are so weak in our faith when God invites us to rest in His strength?

A good verse to memorize and pull out in the midst of intense mocking and ridicule is Isaiah 35:4, which says: "Say to those with anxious heart, 'Take courage, fear not. Behold, your God will come with vengeance; the recompense of God will come, but He will save you.'" They were God's words to Israel in a time of destruction and despair, and they are God's words to you in your own moments of destruction and despair.

God does vindicate His own. He always has and He always will. If we keep our faces firmly set toward the cross, in the end we will receive deliverance from the Lord. It may not always be the deliverance we are expecting, though. Many martyrs have died for their faith.

THE CROSS IS NOT JUST FOR MARTYRS

But this book is not written for those who will die for Christ. Instead, it is written for those who will dare to spend their whole lives living for Him. Part of being a girl who serves means serving God no matter the cost—and there will be a cost. You can count on it. But many times those who set their faces toward the cross can't even see the cost—they can only see Jesus. And if we make a commitment to look for Jesus first in all situations in life, we won't see the cost either.

Someone once said, "Pain plants the flag of reality in the fortress of the rebel heart."[2] We might not all literally die for our faith—but *we will all fight a war.* And in that war we will all incur wounds that will leave ugly scars that are anything but feminine and pretty.

You will not always be popular. You will not always have a big group of friends standing behind you and supporting you in what is right. You will not always have everything you ever wanted. And life will not always be easy. But that is never a reason to quit. You're a soldier. And those in God's army do not get to retire until they go home to be with Him.

There is a story of a World War I soldier who was so distraught with the war that he deserted his fellow troops and attempted to find his way to the coast so he could catch a boat back home to England. In the darkness of the night he stumbled upon a road sign, but it was too dark for him to see what it said. So he climbed up to the top of it and struck a match and found himself looking right into the face of Jesus—he had climbed an outdoor crucifix!

In shock, he began to feel ashamed for forsaking his fellow men when Christ never once forsook him. The next morning that soldier was back in the trenches.[3] Should we ever find ourselves weary enough to quit, we need only look in the face of Jesus, like that soldier did, to keep us going.

Learning the Art of Serving

This book is about many things. It's about learning to hear God's voice and go where He has called you to go. It's about finding your gifts and using them for His glory. It's about being willing to take a lesser position or fight for Christ on the battle-field of life. It's about learning when to serve by doing and when to serve by resting in God's presence. It's about reaching out to those beneath you with kindness and compassion. It's about being willing to be a part of a miracle by offering God all that you have. And it's about watching Him move mountains and knock down walls for those who go forward in obedience. Most important, it's about *finding your life by giving it away*.

By now you know that *Being a Girl Who Serves* is not about one action we may take here or there. It's about living a lifestyle of boldness and audacity, and dying to self. It's about living for more than just you. It's about putting Jesus first, others second, and yourself last. And if you take the first letter from all three of those words, you spell out the word JOY.

That's what being a girl who serves *always* results in. That's why martyrs can die with smiles on their faces. It's why persecuted Christians can sing in prison. It's why young girls from around the world send me e-mails about living for Christ and how doing so is always worth it.

In life you will encounter many opportunities to serve, but you will only get one chance to live. When it is all said and done, will it be said that you were a girl who served? Will you be one who is willing to follow Christ all the way to the cross?

FOR FURTHER THOUGHT:

1. What are some of the things you think your faith might cost you?

2. Would you say you are a different person at school than you are at home or at youth group? Why or why not?

3. What are some difficult things you have had to endure for your faith? How did you respond?

4. Who are some real-life examples of people who have gone all the way to the cross for their faith?

5. What does being a girl who serves mean to you?

TAKING THE CHALLENGE:

Make a public stand for what you believe. You do not have to be "preachy" in your approach. Just simply hold firm to your convictions wherever you are, without considering what the cost to you might be. Remember, joy comes by putting yourself last!

Notes

1. Misty Bernall, *She Said Yes* (Farmington, PA: The Plough Publishing Group, 1999), 114.
2. As quoted in Charles Swindoll's *The Tale of the Tardy Ox Cart* (Nashville, TN: Word Publishing, 1998), 471.
3. Ibid., 169.

BEING A GIRL WHO SERVES

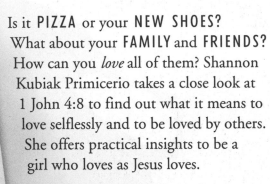

Are you willing to answer the call?

How Mary changed her world—and You can too

GOD CALLED A GIRL

SHANNON KUBIAK

GOD HAS CALLED ON YOU TO MAKE A DIFFERENCE IN THE WORLD. You think you're too average to be God's choice? Mary thought she was average, yet when God came to her with a monumental task, she agreed without hesitation. Never mind the fact that being a pregnant, unwed teen in her day was punishable by death. Mary, a simple, insignificant girl, was just a teenager when she revolutionized society and changed the world. God is looking for world changers. God has big plans for your life; see what He can do with just one person fully committed to Him.

God Called A Girl by Shannon Kubiak

✒ BETHANYHOUSE